D1503402

Lost Innocence

A Daughter's Account of Love, Fear and Desperation

By

Cathy Brochu

ISBN: 0-75962-682-0

This book is printed on acid free paper.

1stBooks - rev. 4/6/01

Acknowledgments

After many years of earnest effort, concession, frustration and perplexity, the book that was once a dream is **published** and available in bookstores everywhere. I wish to take a moment to recognize and pay tribute to those who believed it was possible.

To Theresa Benderson-Mohamed, those Sunday mornings spent talking and dreaming about this book. Thank you for your encouragement, enthusiasm and support.

To Suzane Piela, throughout the writing of this book I so much appreciated your witty sense of humor, guidance, support and sisterhood. Bless you.

To Patty Walsh, Cherie Ackerson, Debbie Cosbey, Diane Dooley-Bryan and Michael Casler, for the time each of you spent reading the rough draft, for your honesty, laughter and tears. I thank you.

Thank you to Tim and Sandy Strack, for the fun filled evening of taking those pictures and then, choosing the right one.

Thank you to Grant LeSchander of Computer Gallery, for your willingness to print the manuscript on demand.

Thank you to Barbara Rossomano, for your support and extraordinary work of creating the web page.

And lastly, to God. From whom, my strength, endurance, love and faith are drawn.

Dedication

This book is dedicated to my mom, Joan Brochu. It was in giving birth to me that the Lineage of incest within our family would one day, come to an end. The cycle would be broken.

From the Readers

"Although I heard all to many cases involving incest and child abuse during my twelve-year tenure as a Family Court Judge in New York State it was the exception-rather than the rule-to hear their stories directly from the child-victims. The law permitted, and usually the adults involved agreed, sparing the child the further trauma of relating, before strangers and before their parents, testimony, which they had inevitably had, had to give repeatedly before the case got to court. <u>Lost Innocence</u> is a harrowing, first-hand account of a child's confusion, helplessness and hope-lessness, which speaks to the pain and insidious impact of sexual abuse in a way no formal or legal indictment or proceeding can. It should be required reading for everyone involved in dealing with incest–judges, lawyers, social workers and perpetrators."

Minna R. Buck,
retired Family Court Judge
Syracuse, New York

"A deeply moving and disturbing story. I could not put it down once I started reading. Presented through the eyes of a child, the narrative had a profound emotional impact on me; upsetting but hopeful. For anyone who works in the field this is a must read."

Nick Pallotta, MSW
Syracuse, New York

"A touching prologue to a personal account of one women's quest for wholeness. At times painful to digest, but a truly honest reflection of the reality that far too many of our society's children must face. A must read for those of us hoping to understand the multi-layered life's of those who experience incest. Thank you to Ms. Brochu for having the courage to share her journey and continuing to help others find their voice!"

Deborah J. Truex, CSW
Syracuse, New York

"This is an incredibly insightful and very personal account of child abuse. The author's simple, straight-forward; first-hand account provides powerful insight into the physical, psychological and emotional effects of child abuse. It is a must read for anyone who works with children in health care, mental health or social work field. Although at times uncomfortably frank, it will leave readers feeling better for having read it. It left me with an uncontrollable need to hug my own children and keep them safe."

Steve Harris, MS
Department of Family Medicine
Upstate Medical University
Syracuse, New York

"Cathy Brochu shares with her readers the agonizing story of her childhood of abuse in this compelling child's-eye narrative. By trusting us with her private pain, she unveils a public issue crying for attention. This book is an important piece of Brochu's many faceted efforts to transform her difficult childhood into a happy childhood for other children. It is a courageous statement of healing and a challenge for us all."

Diane R. Swords,
former Executive Director
Peace Action of Central New York
Syracuse, New York

"The heartfelt voice of a child reaches out to the reader off the pages of <u>Lost Innocence</u>. Her voice is filled with loss, confusion and fear but rises with promise, hope and healing. As you join this child on her captivating traumatic journey, she leads you to understand that survival and recovery are possible even in the face of tragedy. Through her innocent words, the author offers the reader a life-affirming experience of recovery and a sense of hope that all victimized children can reclaim their lives and esteem following trauma."

Jennifer Cornish Genovese,
ACSW, CSW
Psychotherapist, specializing in
the treatment of abused children
Syracuse, New York

"**<u>Lost Innocence</u>** is so valuable and special to the professional field of child abuse prevention. The author is to be firmly commended, and even loudly applauded, for her strength to break the silence of incest. Alice Miller, in the classic **The Drama of the Gifted Child** (formerly **Prisoners of Childhood**) states that the victims of child sexual abuse have been "condemned to silence." This author was condemned to silence in the guise of being special. Ms. Brochu's account reveals how sexual abuse includes components of emotional and physical abuse. An adult has taken advantage of a child's innocence, desire to please and need to be loved resulting in physical violation and damaging emotional confusion. This book will encourage other survivors of child sexual abuse to find the strength to speak out the truths of their own past. It will also encourage our community of professionals and general public to finally accept the prevalence of incest in today's world."

Tamara Henry-Kurtz,
Executive Director
Madison Family Outreach
Center for the Prevention of Child
Abuse and Neglect
Madison County, New York

"A haunting expose' of fragile humanity; its failures and successes. As an attorney practicing in Family Court for twenty-six years, I found the reading of this book a much too unfortunate truth."

John Lindauer, Attorney at Law
Syracuse, New York

Table of Contents

Author's Notes

Innocence is our innate birthright. It knows no cultural or religious boundaries, but is a precious gift to treasure and honor. It holds the magic of our youth and provides wings to explore.

When taken away without permission through incest, it leaves a heart that is an empty shell, untrusting, shamed, fearful and stripped of self-esteem. Lives are shattered, wounds become deep.

There is hope. Recovery is possible. Hearts can be restored. Innocence can be reclaimed. Lives can be rich and fulfilling. I know, because I am a woman who lived the despair of a lineage of incest and I came out the other side, happy, healthy and whole.

My story is shared to present the possibility for others to come out of their silence and discover the beauty of being alive again. My hope is that the shroud of secrecy in our society around the issue of incest be lifted, so we can begin a cultural healing that is long over due.

The book is written from my perspective as a child, in a child's language in order to capture the experience that was my reality at a young age. The book is also written with the hope that it will heighten individuals, families and communities awareness to the prevalence of incest.

The book is based on my life from the age of fifteen-months through sixteen.

Just as my life seemed to unfold in three stages, so will the telling of my story through a series of three books: *Lost Innocence*, *New Beginnings* and *Beyond Survival*. *Lost Innocence* is the first in my trilogy.

Chapter One

Gains and Losses

On October 8, 1955, in Fallriver, Massachusetts, I awaken in a crib, which is gray, made of something hard, and it feels cold. I try to stand up. Something is over the top of the crib, a net. I sit down, looking around. The room's not dark, but bright. I stare through the bars of the crib, looking for my mommy. I call out for her; but she doesn't answer, so I begin to cry.

I hear a noise, footsteps. Again, I call out for mommy. I can see someone walking towards me. The person is dressed in white and has a funny looking hat on her head. As the person gets closer, I say, "Mommy." A strange woman takes the net off the top of the crib. She reaches for me, picking me up, speaking softly and slowly. I cry, but she tells me everything will be "okay."

This woman holds me tightly in her arms and walks around the room, placing my head on her shoulder and wrapping her arms around me. She talks to me, but doesn't sound or smell like my mommy. She walks to the other side of the room. I see another crib, where she stands with me in her arms and says, "Your brother is fine."

I ask for mommy, and begin to cry. She speaks softly to me, saying everything will be "okay."

Today, my mother who is twenty years old, died of Polio; Junior is six weeks old; I am fifteen months. I have lost my best friend, protector and guardian angel. Our lives are about to change in ways that our young minds could not begin to fathom.

We move to Syracuse, New York in the spring of 1958, when I am three and a half years old. What starts off, as an innocent request would soon turn into a nightly routine.

I'm not so sure I like the apartment. Dad and Junior get to share the bedroom and both have their own beds. I don't have a bedroom, nor my own bed! I have to sleep in front of the window in the living room on the pull out couch that turns into a bed. The kitchen is small with barely enough room for the kitchen table. The bathroom has a big tub that stands on funny looking legs. I haven't seen a tub like this before now. It looks like it will be fun to take a bath. There is a long hallway leading into an enclosed porch. I'm excited about this; we can use it as our playroom. Maybe now, Dad won't yell at us as often, for making so much noise when we play.

Junior is running around the apartment; he goes from one room to the other and looks much more excited about the move than I am.

I walk back into the living room, sit on my soon to be bed, look out the window and see people below. I think to myself, "This won't be so bad. I have my own window."

It's the first night, sleeping in the apartment. I'm in my new bed. I have a nightly routine before going to sleep that consists of saying my prayers and talking to God. The apartment is dark and quiet. As I begin my prayers, I hear a noise. So I lay in my bed and listen. I hear it again, get scared, cry, then I scream out for Dad.

He comes to my bed with concern in his voice and asks, "What's wrong?"

I say, "I'm afraid. I want to sleep in your bed."

Dad picks me up with his strong arms and carries me to his bedroom. We lay on the bed, and he holds me close.

2

I can feel the hair from his chest on my face, as he rubs my back. I'm no longer scared, but feel safe. Dad puts his hand between my legs. He rubs it up and down. It feels funny having his hand there, but I say nothing and fall asleep. I awaken the next morning, look for Dad and wonder, "Where is he?" I get scared and yell for him.

Dad hurries into the room and asks, " What's wrong?"

I whimper, "I'm scared."

He looks down at me and says, "You're okay."

This is the first of many nights to come I would sleep with Dad. It would become as natural and routine as saying my prayers or talking to God.

Aunt Cecilia watches us during the day, while Dad is at work. She lives only a couple blocks away from our house. Although she is married, we rarely see her husband. He supervises the construction of the Route 81 overpass that is being built, always goes to work early in the morning and doesn't get home until late. I've only seen him a few times, when we've gone to their house for dinner on the weekend. I like him; he doesn't sit at the kitchen table and talk the entire time we are there, like Dad and Aunt Cecilia. Instead, after dinner and before we go home, he gets down on the floor with both Junior and I, plays with us, laughing and joking. I wish he were home more often, when we're at the house.

Aunt Cecilia has red hair, green eyes, and I am told she looks like my mom. I secretly wish I could stay at her house all the time. When I am with her, I feel special and loved. Today, she teaches me how to play hopscotch. It takes me a while to catch on, but I get it. We laugh and have so much fun. Quite often, she tells Junior and I how much she loves us. I like it, when she tells me that; those simple words make me feel so warm and fuzzy inside.

Directly across the street from Aunt Cecilia's apartment is the County Hospital. Often, I can see the flashing lights and hear the siren from the ambulances that go to and from there. I get scared, cry, and Aunt Cecilia runs to me. She picks me up, wrapping her arms around me, saying, "It's okay."

My fear disappears, and I stop crying, as I hold onto to her, looking into her eyes I say, "I love you."

She squeezes me and whispers, "I love you, too."

Often times, shortly after Aunt Cecilia begins to watch us, when Dad comes to pick us up, instead of leaving right away to go home, Junior and I are given toys to play with in the living room. I don't mind at all; I like being able to play there. Dad and Aunt Cecilia go into the bedroom and stay for what seems to be a long time. When they finally come back out into the living room, where we're playing, I know it's time to go home.

Dad rushes us to pick up the toys. "Come on. Let's go home!"

I run to Aunt Cecilia, give her a big hug and kiss, then smile and say, "I will see you in the morning."

Most nights, I lay in bed, waiting for Dad to come for me. I sleep with him almost every night now. He waits, until Junior is fast asleep, then comes for me, picking me up with his strong arms and carrying me into his bedroom. I lay next to him, feeling so special. I've begun to enjoy the warm sensation I feel throughout my body, when he is rubbing his hand up and down between my legs. It no longer feels foreign or uncomfortable.

Tonight while I am in Dad's bed, he says, "You must not tell anyone what we do."

I don't know what he means so I ask, " Why?"

He turns his head, looks at me and says, "I'll get into trouble."

"What kind of trouble?"

He answers, "They will take you away."

"Where?"

His voice has changed, he sounds mad and then says, "Away from me."

I start to cry, "I don't want to be taken away."

Dad pulls me close and hugs me, "You are my special little girl."

I wrap my arms around him, hold him tight and say, "I love you, Dad. I won't tell anyone. I promise!"

It is at the tender age of five that I begin to fear losing Dad. What would I do without him? Who would take care of me? If they take Dad away, who would love me? I won't tell anyone we sleep in the same bed. I won't tell anyone what we do. God took mom away. I won't let anyone take dad away, but will keep my promise and tell no one.

Junior and I spend our weekends, playing with our many toys or watching television. On nice days we play outside in the front yard. On days when it is too cold outside, we stay on the enclosed porch. Quite often, we imitate cowboys and Indians. I like to pretend I am the Indian by putting on my headband, taking my bow and arrow in my hand; I run around and make attack sounds, like the Indians do on television. Junior pretends he is the cowboy. He puts his cowboy hat on, his holster, then his cowboy boots. We play for hours and have so much fun.

Dad spends most of his time in front of the television on the weekend. Sometimes, he gets upset with us, because we make so much noise, playing. He yells and tells us to quiet down. Neither one of us pay any attention to him, because we know he won't get up off the chair to find out what we're doing.

Today, I pretend I am a grown up and make a cake for us in my easy bake oven. Although it is not a real one, I can bake cakes in it. I mix the ingredients in the bowl, put it all in a small pan, then place it in the oven. I push the button and the light from the oven comes on. I wait patiently for it to go off. I know, when the light goes off, the cake is done. The one I have baked today is the best I have ever made. It smells and tastes good, not dry like the other ones I have made, but moist.

Junior usually complains about my cakes. "It tastes funny." Today, he doesn't complain at all. We sit in our playroom, eating the cake from the pan. When we finish, I notice there isn't a crumb to be found.

I'm six years old. It's a warm summer day. Junior and I are in the living room of Aunt Cecilia's apartment, playing with our toys. I hear footsteps, the door opens, and Aunt Cecilia's husband walks in. I glance up at him.

He looks down at me and asks in a very serious voice, "Where is Aunt Cecilia?"

I tell him, "Dad and Aunt Cecilia are in the bedroom."

He walks towards it and opens the door, yelling, swearing, and telling Dad, "Get out!"

Dad walks out of the bedroom and stands in the dining room. He is trying to talk to my uncle, who has a knife in his hand. He's waving it in the air.

I'm scared. I can feel my body shaking.

He glares at Dad. "Get out, or I will kill you!"

I'm sitting on the floor, and start to cry. I don't know what to do. Junior starts to cry. Dad walks towards us. He bends down, picks us up and walks towards the door. I hold on to him tightly. I look for Aunt Cecilia. I don't see her. I can feel Dad's body shaking, as he carries us down the stairs to the car. He looks upset and scared. Dad doesn't say a word all the way home, neither do Junior or I.

Once we are home, Dad says, "Go play on the porch."

Neither one of us asks any questions; we do as he asks. Dad doesn't say much at dinner; we eat, take a bath and go to bed.

I sleep in my bed tonight. Dad doesn't come for me. I wonder if he's mad at me? No, he can't be, because I didn't do anything wrong, or maybe I did? I'm the one who told that he and Aunt Cecilia were in the bedroom. I begin to cry. I can feel the warmth from my tears rolling down my cheeks. I don't understand why everyone was so upset earlier. I didn't mean to get Dad into trouble. Maybe, if I talk to God, he will make everything better. I say my prayers and ask God, "Please, make everyone happy."

The next morning, we sleep in. Dad doesn't get us up early. Today is only Wednesday. The three of us are sitting at the kitchen table, eating breakfast. Dad still looks sad.

I look up from my cereal bowl and ask, "When are we going to Aunt Cecilia's?"

Dad doesn't look at me, but says, "You're not."

I sit at the table. I don't understand. I asked God to make everyone happy. I look up at Dad and ask, "Why?"

"I have to find a baby sitter."

God, why won't he look at me?

I stare at him and say, "Aunt Cecilia can watch us."

"No."

I insist, "I want to see Aunt Cecilia!"

He answers in a very stern voice, "Stop it!"

Dad has never used this tone of voice before now. I can tell he is upset. I look down at my cereal bowl. I know better than to say another word.

A couple days have passed. Dad tells us he has found a baby sitter, Mrs. Mancini who only lives a couple blocks away. I'm not real excited; I don't want a new baby sitter. I want Aunt Cecilia to watch us.

It's also been a couple days since I've popped the question so I ask, "When will I see Aunt Cecilia?"

He looks at me and says, "I don't know."

I start to cry; Dad picks me up. I put my head on his shoulder, I wrap my arms around him and say, "I miss Aunt Cecilia."

He says, "Me too."

It would be more than a decade later during a time of much confusion, pain, and turmoil in my life that I would be reunited with Aunt Cecilia. She would once again bring me joy and happiness, along with the discovery of my family roots.

It is Sunday afternoon. Tomorrow will be our first day with Mrs. Mancini. Dad has decided to take us to the ice cream parlor that is a short distance from the house. I think he is doing this, because he knows I am sad. Ice cream always makes me feel better, when I'm sick. Today, I'm hoping it will take away the sadness I feel.

I'm sitting on the stool at the counter; Dad twirls me around, while we wait patiently for our order to be taken. I ask for a root beer float and watch the person make it. First, the ice cream goes into the very tall glass; then the root beer is poured over the top of it; and it fizzes. Once my soda float is placed in front of me, I use the straw to drink it, then my spoon to make sure I get all the ice cream out of the glass. The soda float was good. The sadness I felt earlier isn't as strong, but continues to linger within me.

This is our first day with Mrs. Mancini, who is an older lady; her hair is black with streaks of gray; she is short and reminds me of Aunt Jemima. Mrs. Mancini likes to talk. She has an accent and tells me she is Italian. I didn't think I would like her, but I do.

School will be starting in just a few short weeks, and I will be entering the first grade. We spend the remainder of our summer days with Mrs. Mancini, playing with our many toys.

On nice days we go out into the front yard to play. I like being outside. Mrs. Mancini sits on the grass, playing with Junior and I. She tells us stories and always laughs, when we do silly things, she tells us, "You are so cute." Today, Mrs. Mancini picks dandelions from her front yard.

I ask her why she does this?

She turns looks at me, smiles and then tells me that she cooks and eats them.

I look at her and ask; "Don't you know dogs go to the bathroom out here?"

She laughs, "I wash and boil these, before I eat them."

I smile and say nothing, but think to myself, "I hope she never feeds them to us."

The school year has begun, and I'm excited. Before leaving Mrs. Mancini's house for school in the morning, she always gives me a hug and kiss. I like the new school clothes Dad bought me, but I like the hug and kiss I get from her even more. In some ways, she reminds me of Aunt Cecilia. She, too, makes me feel special and loved. Junior is in kindergarten and only has a half-day of school. He and I walk home together in the afternoon.

When we return to Mrs. Mancini's house after school, she always asks, "Did you have a good day?"

I always answer, "Yes."

She has a snack ready for us on the kitchen table, fresh cookies she had baked, while we were at school. I not only like her hugs and kisses, but also love her cookies. When Dad arrives to pick us up, we are either outside playing or inside listening to a story Mrs. Mancini is reading.

Today, when dad arrives to pick us up, he is in a rush and expects her to stop reading. She makes it very clear to him she will complete the story, before we leave. He never again rushes her, when she is reading to us. Instead, when he arrives and she is reading, he stands and listens, until the story is over. Before I leave to go home with dad, she always wraps her arms around me and gives me a big hug and kiss. I know tomorrow will come, and along with it will be a hug and kiss.

In the fall of 1961, I'm seven years old. Mrs. Mancini's greets us at the door, asks us to take our coats off, and sit at the table, so she can talk to us. She doesn't look happy. I notice there are no milk or cookies waiting for us. I wonder what could be wrong? I wonder if I am in trouble?

Mrs. Mancini sits at the table, looks at me and says, "I won't be able to watch you after today."

I don't understand. How can this be? What does she mean?

I ask, "Why?"

"Your father."

I look at her fighting back the tears and ask, "What do you mean?"

"Oh, nothing." Mrs. Mancini doesn't offer any other information.

I begin to cry, look at her and say; "I want you to watch us!"

Mrs. Mancini pulls her chair close to Junior and I. She puts her arms around us, tells us how much she loves us, and lets us know she will miss us.

The words that have just been spoken don't make me feel better. I am very sad; first I lose mom, then Aunt Cecilia, and now I am losing her. "This is not fair!"

Mrs. Mancini sits with her arms wrapped around us, for what seems to be a long time. She let's us know she has made some "special" cookies. She gets up from her chair, goes to the counter, picks up a plate, and places it in the middle of the table. I reach for a cookie, hoping it will help ease the sadness within me.

I hear a knock at the door. It must be Dad. Mrs. Mancini says, "Come in."

Dad walks in the door, looks at us and says in a very stern voice, "Get your coats on, and hurry up!"

Mrs. Mancini helps us gather our belongings, then helps us with our coats. She does this slowly, almost as if she doesn't want us to leave. She walks us to the door.

Dad looks at her and says, "Good bye." He walks out the door ahead of us.

Mrs. Mancini bends down and gives Junior a hug and a kiss; he walks out the door, following a short distance behind Dad.

I stand in the doorway and look up at Mrs. Mancini. I want to cry but hold back the tears. She bends down and embraces me. I don't want her to let go of me; I want to stay in her arms forever. I feel her gentle kiss on the top of my head. God, I don't want to leave. But I know I must. I pull away, look up at her and say, " I will miss you."

I turn and walk out the door.

When we get into the car, there is silence. No words are spoken all the way home. Dad fixes dinner gets us ready for bed, then tells us we will be moving to the country on the weekend. I don't understand. It seems like every time I get close to someone, something happens. I'm beginning to think that maybe I am the one that causes the problem, except no one ever gets mad or upset at me. Dad is the one with whom people get upset.

I crawl into bed. I'm talking to God, telling him I miss mom, Aunt Cecilia, and now I am missing Mrs. Mancini. Before I finish my prayers, Dad comes to get me. He picks me up with his strong arms and puts me in his bed. I don't like it, when he comes to get me, before I finish my prayers. I like the time I spend with God each night. I don't have to give or do anything to God; he just listens. I don't bother to tell Dad how I feel; I'm not sure he would understand, and I don't want to take a chance on him getting mad at me. After all, Dad is just as important to me as God. I talk to God, but Dad takes care of me.

Although I never do see Mrs. Mancini again, she would forever be etched in my memory for her kindness, hugs and gentle kisses. On those rare occasions that I have the opportunity to indulge in home made chocolate chip cookies, I think of her and smile.

Chapter Two
From the Couch to the Bed

Along with the move to the country come changes, some good and some not so good. It's funny; not so long ago, I looked forward to spending time with Dad at night. At the tender age of seven, I no longer feel I have possession of my body. I feel owned. Our nightly routine is no longer fun or enjoyable. Dad doesn't whisper in my ear any more; and when he touches me, it doesn't feel good.

Although the upstairs apartment we live in is small, I like it. I have my own room and very own bed. The nights of having to sleep on a pullout couch are over. Dad and Junior share the bedroom down the hall from mine. The bathroom is right across the hall from my room. This is good. I won't have to walk very far, if I need to go in the middle of the night. The kitchen is small with just enough room for appliances and a table. The living room is the biggest room. It is spacious, even with the large couch we have. Two large windows allow the sun to shine in each morning. Often times, I will stand at one of the windows, allowing the morning sun to touch my face, while I watch the horses grazing across the road.

It all begins shortly after the move. When dad and I are on the couch, he pulls me close and begins to play with my nipples. He rubs them up and down, back and forth.

I don't like the way it feels, but say nothing. He pulls my hand to his penis. I touch it; it's hard, warm, and the skin is soft. "God, it feels so big, I've never touched it before."

He tells me to squeeze it. I squeeze. He instructs me to squeeze it harder, and I do as he asks. It gets harder and harder and has gotten bigger.

He says, "Put it in your mouth."

I don't want to put it in my mouth, but I do it. My mouth is on it. I don't like the smell, and I don't like the taste. I try to pull my head up, but Dad puts his hand on the back of my head and pushes down. I can't get my mouth off of it. This awful tasting stuff comes out of it. I have no choice, but to swallow.

After it's all over, Dad tells me I'm "special."

I don't feel special, but dirty; and I don't like the taste that lingers in my mouth.

As I lay next to him, I hear him say, "You look like your Mom."

I don't understand what he means! What does looking like mom have to do with him putting his penis in my mouth? Doesn't he know how awful it tastes and smells? He picks me up and carries me to my bed. His arms feel warm wrapped around me. He puts me in bed, pulls the covers up over me, and says, "I love you."

I hear the words and quickly forget about the awful taste in my mouth.

He bends down kisses me on the forehead; as he is walking out of the bedroom, he says, "Good night."

I lay in bed, not liking the taste I have in my mouth. The stuff that came out of his penis tastes so bad. I want to get up and brush my teeth, but decide not to. I lay in bed, thinking about how big his penis is. I wonder, if I am going to have to put it in my mouth all the time. God, I hope not!" I'll tell Dad I don't like it. No, I can't; I don't think he would understand. I finally fall asleep. When I awaken in the morning, I make a mad dash to the bathroom, first to brush my teeth, then to go pee.

Spending time with dad on the couch is short lived. He begins to come to my room nightly. Often times, he has me lay on my back. God, I hate when I have to do this! He's on his knees over my body, and all I can see is his penis. He puts it in my mouth and starts shaking it.

I can't move; he makes noises; I taste that awful stuff; I swallow, then it's over.

Tonight, dad does something different. Instead of making me swallow that awful stuff, he pulls it out of my mouth and squirts it on my chest. I smell the familiar smell and am grateful I don't have to swallow it. After he leaves my room, I touch my chest. It feels sticky. I feel dirty. Using the top sheet of my bedding to wipe my chest off, I then kick it to the bottom of the bed. I don't want it near me.

On those days when Junior and I aren't at school or the baby sitters, we can be found with Dave and Linda. They live in the house next door and we rent our apartment from their parents, Jim and Virginia. Together, the four of us learn to climb trees, ride bikes, build tree houses and manage to get ourselves into trouble from time to time. Where you would find one of us, you would find the others. Jim and Virginia call us the four musketeers.

On a warm Saturday afternoon, Linda and I are in the backyard, playing catch. Dad sits, watching us and holding his cup of coffee in one hand and cigarette in the other. It's unusual for him to sit and watch us play. Today, I get mad at him. After Linda and I finish playing catch, we walk over to where he is sitting.

Dad looks at Linda and says, "You're such a pretty little girl."

I can't believe he has said this to her. I'm supposed to be his special little girl! I look at Linda; she has a smile on her face.

I look at Dad, and he says, "Come here."

I walk towards him, then notice the warmth of my tears rolling down my face. I hadn't noticed, until that moment I was crying. Dad reaches for me. I reach for him. I feel his arms wrap around me, and I hold onto him. I can't stop crying.

Dad whispers in my ear, " You will always be my special little girl, now stop crying and go play."

His gentle touch and words are comforting. I quickly forget about the jealousy that I felt a few moments ago.

I wipe my face with my hands, turn towards Linda, and say, " Lets go ride our bikes."

Every so often on the weekend, I see Dave and Linda playing outside with their dad. I watch from a distance. They wrestle, laugh, hug one another and seem to be having so much fun. I wish, dad would spend time, playing with me outside. It seems the only time he and I have physical contact with one another is at night. These days I don't know what to expect, when he comes to my room. Quite often, he has me do something different each night. I no longer look forward to the time we spend with one another. Instead, I begin to dread it.

One of the things I really don't like is when he walks into the room with a jar of Vaseline. He doesn't have to tell me anymore what to do. I stick my finger in the jar; he's on his back. I put my finger up his butt, and move it in and out. God, how I hate doing this! It's finally over. He leaves my room.

My finger is greasy and smells. I use the top sheet of the bedding to wipe the Vaseline and poop from my finger.

The Vaseline comes off, but I'm stuck with the awful odor that is left on my finger. I stick my hand under the pillow and wait for morning to come.

My safe haven becomes the visit I make to the horses that are kept in the fenced in area across the road from our house. On my daily visits with them, I talk and they are willing to listen. My four legged friends always seem to enjoy the grass or apple I bring. On those days when I bring nothing, they still stand and listen to what I have to say. I begin to trust and rely on them to listen to my every woe.

Dad thinks it's "silly," I go to see the horse's everyday. Little does he know that along with my daily visit comes comfort and companionship. The four-legged animals quickly become my best friends.

Today, I stand at the fence and look up at them. I can feel the warmth of tears rolling down my cheeks. I tell them about the secrets and promises Dad and I have. I let them know I don't like what he makes me do. The four of them stand there, listening intently, and seem to understand what I am saying. I hear Dad calling me, so I wipe the tears from my cheeks. Before running across the road, I look at each of them and say, "I'll see you tomorrow."

Chapter Three

A Prayer

In the late summer of 1962, we travel to Schenectady, New York. The time spent with Aunt Betty, Uncle Jack, and my cousin Claudette would be filled with fun, laughter and the discovery that some prayers are answered. I realize at the age of eight I need to think long and hard before I pray.

The drive to their house is long and boring. I sit in the back seat, reminiscing about each of them. Aunt Betty is of average size and appearance. She wears glasses and looks a lot like the picture dad showed me of mom a long time ago. It seems she is always attending to everyone else's needs. She speaks comely, softly and never raises her voice. I especially like this about her. My favorite time is when she tucks me into bed at night. She kneels next to me, and we say our prayers. This is a real treat for me; dad and I never pray together. After we finish with our prayers, she pulls the covers up to my chin, kisses me on the forehead, and lets me know she and God love me. I look into her eyes and sense the deep love she has for me.

Uncle Jack gets around in a wheel chair. I'm told he was in the Korean War. A bomb went off, and the end result was his loss of his legs and one arm. In past times, when we have visited, he let me sit on his lap and we went racing around the house. I had so much fun. Although his legs are gone, he is able to maneuver the wheel chair quite well. He always makes homemade spaghetti sauce. It is so good. Maybe, this visit he will let me help.

Although Claudette and I are the same age, we look very different. I am thin and have shoulder length hair. Claudette has dark hair, is overweight, and seems to only speak, when someone speaks to her. We not only look different, but we have different interests. I'd rather be outside climbing a tree or building a fort; she, on the other hand, enjoys playing with her dolls. This is my least favorite thing to do. I find them very boring. Claudette actually talks to the dolls, as if they can hear her. Maybe, this visit I'll get lucky, and she won't ask me to play with those boring things.

Ah, the long drive has ended. As we pull into the driveway, I can see Aunt Betty coming out of the door of their small house. The car stops, and out the door I go, running to her. She bends down reaches for me, and I fall into her arms. Her skin is soft, warm, and the perfume she is wearing has a sweet smell to it. It's good to once again feel her arms wrapped around me. I notice Uncle Jack sitting in his chair.

As I turn to run to him, I yell out, " Uncle Jack, Uncle Jack."

He reaches for me; I reach for him, and we embrace. He comments on how big I've gotten. I walk over to Claudette and give her a hug. She doesn't hug back. I let her know I've missed her, but she doesn't say a word, just stands there, looking at me. I begin to feel uncomfortable; I don't know what else to say. Aunt Betty comes to the rescue and invites us all into the house.

After lunch, Aunt Betty takes us to the park. The three of us pile into the car. I think, she has chosen to do this, because the three of us have so much energy. Once we're there, both Claudette and Junior run to the swings. Rather than following them, I stand in awe, staring at all the trees.

19

Aunt Betty notices and says, "Aren't they beautiful?"

The trees are so big. The leaves are green and the tree trunks, their mammoth.

She tells me this is her favorite park. She goes on to say that whenever she needs to think or pray, this is where she comes.

I take a deep breath, filling my lungs with the fresh air. I move in a circle, continuing to take in all the beauty that surrounds me. It's not difficult to understand why this is her favorite park.

Aunt Betty drops to the grass and invites me to sit on her lap. I don't pass up the invitation. Her arms are wrapped around me. I can feel her breath on the back of my neck. We watch Claudette and Junior playing in the distance. She tells me I look a lot like my mom, when she was my age.

I say, "Really."

In an instant, I am overwhelmed with sadness.

I feel my eyes filling with tears; I try to hold them back, but I'm not able. I start to cry.

She turns me around and asks, "What is wrong?"

I tell her I miss mom a lot and wish she hadn't died.

She tells me Mom isn't very far away.

I look into her eyes and ask, "What do you mean?"

She places her hand over her heart and says, "Your Mom will forever live within your heart."

I tell her I talk to Mom almost every night, after saying my prayers and before going to sleep.

She smiles. "You are so much like your Mom. She prayed every night, too."

Aunt Betty suggests we look up into the sky and say, "Hi, Mom."

I feel silly, because I haven't done this before. The only time I talk to Mom is at night. I guess, it will be okay, Aunt Betty is going to do it with me. We both look up into the sky and on the count of three shout, "Hi."

Evening has finally arrived. I'm glad, because I'm tired. Both Junior and I sleep on the soft red benches that are used during the day in the kitchen. I grab a pillow and blanket from the chair in the living room and announce to everyone that I am going to bed. As I am walking towards the kitchen, Aunt Betty lets me know she will tuck me in shortly. As I lay on the bench, waiting patiently for Aunt Betty, I can hear Junior laughing in the other room and wonder where he gets all his energy. I hear footsteps. It's Aunt Betty.

She kneels next to the bench, makes the sign of the cross and says, "In the name of the Father, Son and Holy Ghost." Then, she begins to pray. She thanks God for the day and asks him to watch over me, while I sleep. She tells God she is thankful I have come to visit and asks that he watch over all our loved ones here and all those who have passed away.

Together we say, "Amen."

She wraps her arms around me, kisses me on the forehead and lets me know she loves me. As she walks out of the kitchen, I hug my pillow and say, "I love you, too."

The next morning, we are all sitting at the breakfast table.

Uncle Jack says, "Cathy, today is Our Day."

I look at him and ask, " What do you mean?"

He announces, "We are going to make homemade spaghetti sauce."

I look at him and say, "Really!" I'm so excited.

Aunt Betty tells Uncle Jack he will need to wait, until she cleans up the kitchen. She suggests Claudette and I go to her room to play.

I look at Claudette. She looks at me and we both walk towards her room.

I think to myself, "Oh no, those boring dolls." Claudette hasn't made her bed yet, so I ask if she would like me to help her.

She says, "Sure."

God, I hope she doesn't ask me to play dolls. We finish making the bed. I hear Uncle Jack calling me from the other room, and I go running.

I hurry into the kitchen, where Uncle Jack lets me know he needs my help. He sits in his wheel chair at the kitchen table. I stand next to him, waiting for my instructions. There are a few bowls on the table, a big pot, fresh mushrooms, onions, and peppers. He tells me to cut up the peppers, placing the peppers on a cutting board, giving me a small knife and instructing me on how to cut them up very small. Before I begin, he warns me to be careful not to cut myself.

I say, "I am a big girl and know I can do this."

He cuts up the onion and tells me, "This sauce is going to be so good."

I tell Uncle Jack, "Your sauce is always good."

He mixes all the ingredients in the big bowl that has the meat in it and says, "You get to make the meatballs. " He instructs me to take a small amount of meat out of the bowl and roll it into a small ball.

Before I know it, the bowl is empty; and a lot of meatballs sit in front of me.

Uncle Jack lets me know the hard part is done. Now everything goes into the pot to cook slowly. He tells me he adds his own spices.

I sit and watch him go from one jar to the next.

He says, "We will add a pinch of this and then a pinch of that."

I laugh. "You are silly. "

He says, "The sauce is ready to go on the stove. Go get Aunt Betty."

I run out into the living room and let Aunt Betty know Uncle Jack needs her help.

She gets right up, follows me into the kitchen and says, "It looks like you two have had fun."

I grin at both Aunt Betty and Uncle Jack. "The sauce is going to be good, because I helped."

They look at one another, chuckle, and Uncle Jack says, "You're right."

I've smelled the sauce all day long and anticipated the taste. I'm hungry and can't wait to eat. I help Aunt Betty get the plates, silverware, napkins and glasses out for dinner, hoping we will eat soon. It's finally time to demolish the food.

I sit patiently at the table, waiting for my spaghetti, meatballs and homemade sauce. I watch Aunt Betty fix my plate. I waste no time, once she places it in front of me. First I go for the meatball. Ah, it tastes so good. I twirl the spaghetti on my fork, then put it in my mouth. The sauce is great.

Dad says, " Jack, you have done it again."

Uncle Jack says, "No, Cathy and I have done it. She is my little helper."

I look at him and smile. I am proud, full and happy.

23

It is our last night at the house. Dad and Aunt Betty have gone to a movie. I'm excited. Uncle Jack is going to read to us. The three of us run into the living room, after brushing our teeth and putting on our pajamas.

I ask Uncle Jack, "Can I sit on your lap?"

He says, "Yes."

Junior begs, "I want to sit on his lap."

I scowl at Junior. "I'm going to sit on his lap."

He pushes me away. "No, I am."

Uncle Jack tells us both to stop, then says, "Cathy, I will give you a ride later."

I look at Junior, call him a baby and tell him with a big smile on my face, "I'm getting a ride later."

After Junior gets on Uncle Jack's lap, he moves his wheel chair up next to the couch, so Claudette and I can see the pictures in the book. I really like it, when he reads to us. He makes sounds and noises; instead of using the names in the book, he uses our names. When he makes his funny noises, the three of us laugh so hard.

I listen intensely as he reads and really feel as if though I am a part of the story. Uncle Jack finishes reading the story.

I ask if he will read another.

He says, "It is late. You need to go to bed, so you are rested for the long ride home tomorrow."

Hugs and kisses are given. Junior grabs a pillow and blanket from the chair in the living room and runs to the kitchen. Uncle Jack rolls himself into the kitchen. I follow a short distance behind him. Junior gets on the bench. Uncle Jack pulls the blanket up over him and says good night.

He turns his wheelchair around, looks at me and says, "Hop on."

I get on his lap. I'm so excited; I finally get my ride. He maneuvers the wheelchair through the kitchen, living room, then into his bedroom. I've not been in his room before. He pulls his chair up next to the nightstand, then tells me to get down. When I'm off his lap, I just stand there.

He looks at me and says, "You are a very special little girl."

I don't know what to say or do.

He tells me he wants to show me something.

I exclaim, "Show me. Show me, Uncle Jack."

He unzips his pants, pulls his penis out and holds it in his hand.

Oh, no, I don't want to do this! I stand there not saying a word.

He reaches for my hand, telling me, "I only want you to touch it." He pulls me closer, guides my hand to his penis, and says, "I won't hurt you. Put your mouth on it."

I stand in silence. My body feels numb. I don't want to put that awful thing in my mouth.

Again, he says, "Put your mouth on it for just a minute."

I put my mouth on it. God, how I hate doing this.

He shakes it, and the awful stuff starts to come out of it. I pull my head up and off his penis. He continues to shake it. I stand there watching him. After it's all over, he reaches for a Kleenex, wipes it off, and puts it back in his pants. He then says, " Come, sit on my lap."

I say, "I am tired and want to go to sleep."

He says, "Hop up on my lap, and I will give you a ride."

I say, "I have to get my pillow and blanket from the living room and want to walk."

He says, "Okay."

I hurry out of his bedroom and into the living room. I'm so glad to be away from him. I grab the pillow and blanket from the chair and head for the kitchen. He's right behind me. I put my pillow down, and lay on the bench. He reaches for the blanket and covers me up. I don't hug him, and I don't say goodnight.

As he is wheeling himself out of the kitchen, I hear him say, "Goodnight."

I lay on the soft red bench. The taste in my mouth is awful. I want to get up to brush my teeth. But, I don't. If I get up, Uncle Jack might ask me to do something else. I start to cry and bury my head in the pillow. I don't want to wake Junior, and I don't want Uncle Jack to hear me. I talk to God and tell him how mad I am. I ask, "Why do I always have to put that thing in my mouth?" I listen for an answer, but all I can hear is Junior breathing. I pray Uncle Jack dies and doesn't go to heaven, because of what he made me do. I hug my pillow and ask God, "Watch over me, until Aunt Betty gets home."

The next day, Aunt Betty says, "Good morning, Sunshine."

I look towards her. "Good morning." I lay on my back for a few minutes and think about last night. I want to tell Aunt Betty what happened, but I know I shouldn't. I don't want to get Uncle Jack into trouble.

Aunt Betty asks, "Are you going to sleep all morning?"

I sit up. "I'm up."

Aunt Betty says, "Come have some juice."

I get up and walk towards the stove, where she is standing and handing me a glass of juice.

She asks, "Did you have fun last night?"

I stand in silence, not knowing what to say.

Junior and Claudette come into the kitchen.

Aunt Betty again asks, "Did you kids have fun last night?"

Junior says, " Yes. Uncle Jack read to us, and I got to sit on his lap."

I say nothing.

Before we begin breakfast, Aunt Betty says a prayer. She asks God to guide and protect us. She thanks Him for the food we are about to eat and says, "Amen." Then, Aunt Betty talks about the movie she and Dad went to see last night, saying it was a real treat for her, because she really never gets out of the house. She goes on to say it has been so much fun for her to have us visit.

Dad asks, "Cathy, why are you so quiet?"

Before I can answer, Uncle Jack says, "She is probably not awake yet."

I look at Uncle Jack, then Dad. I'm wide-awake. I just don't have anything to say to either one of them.

Aunt Betty asks, "Aren't you feeling well?"

I say, "I'm just not very hungry."

Dad glances at Aunt Betty and says, " She's probably sad, because we're leaving."

While Dad loads up the car with our belongings, Claudette and I hang out in her bedroom. All the dolls are neatly placed on the bed. Claudette yells out my name. I turn my head to look at her, hoping she doesn't ask me to play dolls with her, before we leave.

She looks at me and says, "I'm going to miss you."

I notice she has tears in her eyes. I ask her, if she is sad. She looks down at her feet and doesn't say a word.

I say, "Maybe, we can come to visit again, next year."

She looks up at me and says, "Really!"

Junior runs into the room, announcing, "Dad says it is time to go. Come on."

I look at him and say, "Okay. Okay. I'm coming."

We all gather in the living room for the final good byes.

Dad says, "The car's all packed, and we're ready to go."

Aunt Betty and I look at each other, walking towards each other. When she reaches for me, I fall into her arms, crying.

"There is no need to be sad." She hugs me, strokes my hair, and tells me she will write.

"You'll see me next year, God permitting. Now come on. Let me see my pretty girl."

I stand nice and tall and give her one of my big smiles.

Uncle Jack asks, "Am I going to get a good bye hug?" He's sitting in his chair next to the front door.

I was hoping I could avoid saying good bye to him, but I walk slowly over to him.

As I approach, he says, "Give your favorite Uncle a hug."

I think to myself, "You use to be my favorite Uncle, but not any more." I give him a quick hug. I don't squeeze or hold onto him like I've done in the past.

He doesn't ask for a kiss. He wouldn't have gotten one, even if he had asked. He's lucky he got a hug.

I say my good byes to Claudette and run out the door. I sit in the front seat of the car for a few minutes. Dad and Junior finally come out. As we back out of the driveway, Aunt Betty lifts her fingers to her lips and blows me a kiss.

I smile and wave good bye.

I sit in the front seat for the long drive home. Instead of looking out the window at all the cars that pass us, I find myself thinking about Uncle Jack. I wonder if he makes Claudette touch his penis. I wonder if he puts it in her mouth. I don't like what he made me do. Maybe I should have told Aunt Betty. No, I couldn't do that. It would only cause trouble, and then we would never see one another again. I want to see Aunt Betty and Claudette next year. I will tell no one and hope it doesn't happen again.

About six months after our visit, dad receives a letter from Aunt Betty. I am excited and want to know what she has written.

Dad tells me I have to wait for him to read the letter. He sits on the couch and lights a cigarette. I watch and wait patiently for him to finish reading the letter. I see him folding the letter. He must be done.

I ask, "Dad, what did Aunt Betty say?"

He says, "I don't have good news."

I ask, "What's wrong?"

Dad says, "Uncle Jack was very sick and has died."

He has tears in his eyes and looks sad. I remember so clearly the last night I was at Uncle Jack's house. I wished he would die and God wouldn't let him go to heaven. Now, I regret wishing him dead.

I ask Dad, "Can I go outside?"

He answers, "Yes."

I sit on the grass and have a talk with God, crying. I let him know I didn't really want Uncle Jack to die. I ask him to please let Uncle Jack go to heaven. I tell God there were a lot of fun things Uncle Jack and I did. I let him know Uncle Jack only made me do those awful things to him that one night. I ask God to answer this one last prayer. I look up into the sky and plead he send Uncle Jack to heaven. I know now God does answer prayer.

Chapter Four

Disappointment and Confusion

As a family, we had a yearly ritual of returning to the cemetery, where Mom was buried in Fallriver, Mass-achusetts. Dad would combine the trip with a visit to the beach, his friend's restaurant and the amusement park. It would be a time of adventure, fun, laughter, and tears. In yesteryears during our return trip home, I would sit in the back seat, filling my head with thoughts of expectations for next year's trip. July of 1963 would be very different for me. I find myself sitting in the front passenger seat, feeling disappointed and confused.

The amusement park is always so much fun. As I think about it, I can smell the hamburgers and hot dogs cooking and ah, my favorite, cotton candy. Every year, we ask, if we can ride the Roller Coaster, and dad always says, "You are too small."

This year will be different. He tells us, because we are older and bigger, we will be able to ride it.

Both Junior and I are really excited. I can't wait! The beach is my favorite place to go. Although I don't like the taste of the salty water, I enjoy the ocean. I have this game I play. I stand in the water and wait for a wave to come crashing into me. Just before it reaches me, I head for shore. Most times, the wave gets me long before my feet touch the warm sand. On those rare occasions when I make it to shore, I laugh and say, "I did it."

Making a sandcastle with dad and Junior is always so messy, but I don't mind. It seems that each year the sandcastle we create gets bigger and bigger. Running to the water edge, filling the pail, running back and then creating our sandcastle is so much fun. My least favorite time is when we go see dad's friend, who owns a restaurant.

Actually, I don't know his name. He's never impressed me.

Dad tells me that many years ago when I was just a baby, his friend helped him out right after Mom died. He's older, polite and always buys lunch for us. The conversation, which takes place, is between him and dad. He doesn't really talk to me. If he says anything, he comments on how big I've gotten.

I think to myself, "Doesn't he know I'm supposed to grow?" The highlight of the visit to the restaurant for me is always lunch.

Dad on the other hand seems to enjoy himself.

I'm bigger and older now, hoping that this year I won't get scared at the cemetery.

In past times, Junior has told me the statues were going to "get me." I believed him. He would hide behind one of them, jump out and scare me.

I would scream, cry, and run to Dad. This year will be different. I'll show him he can no longer scare me. I now know the statues can't hurt me.

We're at the beach. The sun is shining; it's a warm day, and the summer breeze feels so good on my face. Junior and I are playing in the sand. Dad is sitting next to us, looking out at the water.

I ask, "Help us make a sand castle?"

He laughs.

I ask, "What is so funny?"

31

He tells me, "Your Mom and I use to come to this beach."

I ask, "Did you just come to look at the water?"

Dad says, "We used to play in the sand."

I ask, "Did you make sand castles?"

Dad smiles. "Yes."

The three of us gather sand and put the sand in piles. Dad grabs the pail and instructs us to sit, until he returns. I watch him walk down to the water. He bends down, fills the pail and heads back to us. The three of us spend what seems to be hours, creating our sandcastle.

Once it is complete, dad tells us, "It's the best I've ever seen!"

I look at Dad and smile. I feel so proud and happy.

The three of us are covered with sand from head to toe. Dad suggests we go down to the water to rinse off. As I walk down to the water, holding Dad's hand, I notice the warmth of the sand on my feet. I'm hoping the water is just as warm.

Once we reach the water Dad says, "Come on. Let's get in."

I move towards the water. I stick my foot in, but the water feels cold.

Dad doesn't give me much time to think about whether or not I'm getting in. He picks me up, twirls me around; and before you know it, I'm in the water. The sound of laughter and splashing fill the air.

After leaving the beach and before going back to the Motel, we stop and get something to eat. Both Junior and I pick at our food. All I want to do is go to sleep. I'm so tired.

It's funny; each year when we make this trip, we stay in a motel; the three of us sleep in the same bed. Dad doesn't touch my body or make me do any of those awful things to him. I secretly wish we could make the trip to see mom much more often.

Once we get back to the Motel, I waste no time getting ready for bed. The three of us climb into bed. Junior is on one side of Dad; I, on the other side. I feel Dad's arm wrapped around me.

He asks, "Did you have fun today?"

Without any hesitation I answer, "Yes" and say good-night.

The three of us are nestled in bed for a good night sleep after a fun filled day.

This is the part of the trip to which I least look forward. We are on our way to the restaurant to see dad's friend. He tells us after we visit and have lunch, that we will go to the amusement park. I wish we could just skip the boring visit and go have fun.

We arrive at the restaurant.

Before entering the front door, dad reminds both of us, "Behave."

As we enter, I see dad's friend in the distance. He walks towards us, he has a smile on his face, and as he gets closer he extends his hand to Dad and says, "Hi Manny."

I stand there wondering if or when he is going to notice me. Finally, he looks at us and says, "You children must be hungry. Come sit at a table and let's get you some lunch."

We follow him to the table like well-behaved polite children that we are. I think to myself, "I'm really not interested in food. I want to go to the amusement park."

We've been at the restaurant for what seems to be hours. Both Junior and I have finished our lunch and are quite anxious to leave. Each year when we come to the restaurant to visit, we get to sit at our very own table. When I was younger, I really didn't mind; but now that I am older, I wonder about what he and Dad talk about. I wish our tables were closer, so I could hear what they were saying. Ah, finally, its looks like it might be time to go.

Dad walks over to our table. "We better get going."

Neither Junior nor I waste any time. Before you know it, we're up, out the door and running to the car. I think to myself, "Amusement Park, here we come!"

As we walk from the parking lot to the main gate to get into the Amusement Park, I can see the Ferris wheel. For some reason it doesn't look as big as it was last year. I think to myself, "Maybe it's because I'm bigger." As we stand in line to purchase tickets for the rides, I notice the familiar food smells of past visits. I wish I hadn't eaten so many french-fries at lunch. Hopefully, before we leave, I'll have room for cotton candy.

Once the tickets are purchased, the three of us head to the bumper cars. This has always been my favorite ride. We get into a bright red car. Junior is on one side of Dad; I, on the other. Before you know it, the car is moving. I look around and see that all the cars are filled with other people. I was so excited, when I got into the car I hadn't noticed anyone one else. Someone bumps into us from behind, and it makes our car go faster. I look straight ahead and see the wall, get nervous, and hold onto Dad's leg. We hit the wall, then bounce back out into the middle of the floor.

Junior says, "Get them, Dad, Go faster!"

Dad is able to turn the car around and head for the one that is closest to us. He hits it and we watch it bounce into the wall. I laugh, then notice the laughter coming from the other cars. I realize I'm not the only one having fun.

The big event of the day has finally arrived. We're standing in line to get on the Roller Coaster. As we stand there, I notice that some people, who are on the Roller Coaster, are smiling; others are laughing; still others scream.

I get a little nervous and ask Dad, "Why are people screaming?"

Dad says, "They are having fun."

God, I hope I don't start screaming when we're at the very top.

Junior seems to be very excited and says to Dad, "I can't wait to get on."

I stand, watch and listen. The Roller Coaster has stopped. It's our turn to get into one of the cars. Dad sits in the middle; Junior is on one side, I, on the other side. Dad pulls down the bar.

The man who took our tickets says, "Everyone enjoy and hold onto your hats."

Dad laughs.

I ask, "What is so funny?"

He says, "I hope I don't lose my hat."

I smile. "You won't."

I notice the car is moving and feel nervous as the car begins to move faster. It feels like we're going up a hill. I look over the side and see we are very high in the air. I get scared. I don't ever remember being up so high. I move as close to Dad as I can. I feel his arm touching mine.

Dad says, " We're at the top of the tracks. Hold on."

We begin to descend. The cars are going real fast. I can feel the wind pushing against my face. I hear the people in the car in front of us, screaming.

I get scared, cry and tell Dad, "I want to get off."

Dad says, "Hold on."

I can't stop crying. My stomach feels like it is in my throat, and I feel so sick.

Dad puts his arm around me. "It's okay."

Having his arm around me doesn't make me feel any better. I just want the ride to stop. The car is slowing down and finally comes to a complete stop. Dad lifts the bar, and out of the car I go. As I'm walking down the stairs, I hear Junior ask, "Can I ride it again?"

I think to myself, "No way am I getting back on that ride."

After the ride on the Roller Coaster, Dad decides we need to walk around, rather than go on any other rides. Those words are music to my ears. I don't think I would have been able to get on another ride without getting sick.

After we've walked around the amusement park and played some games for awhile, my stomach feels better. As we walk, I see the cotton candy vendor and think, "Ah, cotton candy."

Dad must be thinking the same thing and asks, " Are you ready for cotton candy?"

Both Junior and I say, Yes."

The cotton candy is just as I remembered it to be sweet, sticky and yummy. As I sit and lick it from my fingers, I think, "What a perfect way to end a perfect day."

On Sunday morning, we go to the cemetery. Dad likes to stop here, before we leave for the long drive home. As the three of us walk along the path that leads to mom's gravestone, I fight back the tears. God, how I miss her. As Dad bends down to place the vase of flowers at the base of the stone, I feel the warmth of tears rolling down my cheeks.

Dad notices and asks, "What is wrong?"

"I don't want you to die."

He bends down, picks me up, and holds me in his arms. I put my head on his shoulder and hold onto him as tight as I can. I don't want to let go. I don't want him to die.

Dad whispers in my ear, "I'm not going to die. I will be with you forever."

I lift my head, look into his eyes and say, " Promise that you will never leave!"

He looks into my eyes and says, "I promise."

I tell him, "I miss Mom."

He says, "I miss her too."

I ask, "Did Mom love me?"

He says, "She loved you very much and talked to you all the time."

I ask, "Was Mom sad, when she was sick?"

He says, "She was very sad."

I ask, "Why?"

He says, "She didn't want to leave me, Junior or you." Dad gives me a hug and puts me down. We both stand in silence, looking down at the gravestone.

I think to myself, "Dad made a promise. I know he'll keep it and never leave me."

Junior yells for me and says, "Let's play hide and seek."

I turn, look for him, but can't see him anywhere. I hear his voice and walk down the path. I'm sure he's hiding behind one of the statues and at any moment is going to jump out and try to scare me. This year it won't work. The statues don't seem to be as big, and I'm not afraid.

Sure enough, he jumps out from behind a statue and says, "It's going to get you." I laugh. "I'm not afraid. It's only a statue and can't hurt me."

The three of us stand at the gravestone to say our good-byes. I look up at dad; he's wiping his face with his hankie and looks sad. I kneel on the soft ground, fold my hands and silently talk to God. I ask that he not let anything happen to dad. I ask that he tell mom how much I miss and love her. Again, I feel the warmth of tears rolling down my cheeks. I feel Dad's hand on my shoulder. I make the sign of the cross and slowly stand.

I'm not able to control the tears or crying.

Dad picks me.

Junior says, "You baby."

Dad looks at him and says, "Shut up."

He holds me a few minutes then says, "We have to go."

As we walk towards the car, I turn, look towards the gravestone and sigh, "I love you, mom."

It's mid-day, and we've begun our journey home. This year is different from past years. I get to sit in the front seat, and Junior gets the back. I'm not sure why Dad has decided this. I think, it's because I'm older. The sound of the soft music playing on the radio is nice. I look over my shoulder and notice Junior is sleeping. My eyelids begin to feel heavy. I rest my head on the door and close my eyes.

"Cathy."

I hear my name and think I'm dreaming.

"Cathy."

I hear my name again, and it sounds like dad. I open my eyes and turn my head towards him. He has one hand on the steering wheel; the other, on his penis. I blink my eyes, thinking that what I'm seeing is not true.

Dad says, "Come here, Cathy."

I move slowly towards him. He holds his penis in his hand and shakes it.

I think to myself, "Oh no, I hope, I don't have to put it in my mouth."

He tells me to shake it. I touch it.

38

He tells me, " Squeeze it."

I squeeze it.

He says, "Shake it."

I'm shaking it; my arm gets sore, and I slow down.

He says, " Shake it faster."

I do as he asks. The awful stuff comes out of it. It's all over my hand.

He reaches for his hankie, then hands it to me.

I wipe the smelly, sticky stuff off my hand.

"You are my special little girl."

I look at dad and say, "I'm tired."

He says, " You can go back to sleep."

I move back over to the passenger's side and sit as close to the door as I can. I close my eyes and hope that Dad thinks I've gone back to sleep.

I sit with my eyes closed, reflecting on the past three days. Dad, Junior and I slept in the same bed, and he didn't touch me. The time spent at the beach and amusement park was so much fun. I think about dad holding me at the cemetery. He took away my sadness and made me feel safe. What I don't understand is if he loves me as much as he says, why does he make me do those things to him. The trip was perfect up to now. Why did he have to ruin it?

This would be the last trip the three of us would make back to the cemetery together. As an adult, I have ventured back to the beach, amusement park and cemetery. As I stand looking down at mom's gravestone I find myself not dwelling on the disappointment and confusion I felt as a child, but remembering the times of adventure, fun and laughter.

Chapter Five
A Warm Summer Day

It really never mattered to me who would baby-sit us, since I spent most of my day outside playing. Today would be different though; I would forever remember the one and only time Loren watched us. The warm, sunny summer day of 1964 would bring with it yet another secret, a secret I would share with no one.

After lunch, Loren lets us know we need to spend an hour or so of quiet time in our rooms. I've not had to do this before, but know not to ask any questions, after all he is the babysitter. I think, the reason he's having us do this is so he can practice playing pool in the front room. If we are in our rooms, at least he knows where we are. A couple nights a week, he and dad play pool, after we go to bed. I would think he would get tired of the game. I lay on my back in my bed, looking up at the ceiling and thinking about being outside. God, it's too nice of a day to be cooped up inside this apartment. I listen for the familiar sound of the balls dropping into the pockets, but hear nothing, except the sound of footsteps coming from the hall leading to my room. The next thing I know Loren is standing in my doorway.

He walks towards my bed. "I am going to take a nap with you."

I feel my body get tense. I don't know what to do or what to say.

He lays next to me, then turns towards me. All I can see is his chest. He takes my hand, puts it between his legs and rubs it up and down. I can feel it. It's hard.

I think to myself, "Oh, no!"

He pulls my hand to his penis.

It feels big, warm and hard. I don't want to touch it. I don't want to do this. I try to pull my hand away, but he puts his over mine and guides it to his penis.

Oh God, please, I don't want to put it in my mouth.

With his hand over mine he begins to shake it faster and faster; it gets harder, then the awful stuff comes out of it.

As he lays next to me, I think, "God, I just want to get up and run out of the house."

A few minutes pass before he looks at me and says, " If you tell your father, you will get into trouble."

I start to cry. "I don't want to get into trouble."

He says, "You won't if you keep your mouth shut." He gets up, puts his penis in his pants, and says, "When Junior wakes up, we can go outside."

He turns walks out of the room and down the hall. A few minutes pass before I hear the familiar sound of a ball falling into one of the pockets. He must be playing pool.

I can't stop crying. I bury my head in the pillow and ask, "Why do I always have to do these things?" I talk with God and tell him, "I don't like what Loren made me do." I let him know I am tired of having to keep secrets. I listen and think that maybe I will hear God's voice. But the voice I hear is Junior's.

He walks into my bedroom and says, "Come on. Let's go outside to play."

I get up off my bed and walk into the kitchen where I stand by the table and ask Junior, "Where is Loren?"

He says, "He's in the living room."

41

I whisper, so Loren can't hear me and say, "Ask if we can go outside."

He walks into the living room. I hear him ask, "Can we go outside?"

I hear Loren say, "Yes."

I don't waste any time getting out of the house. I turn, open the door and run down the stairs. I'm hoping Loren stays in the house and doesn't come outside. I don't want him near me.

A few minutes later, both Junior and Loren walk down the stairs that lead to the back yard.

Junior yells to me, "Let's play ball."

Normally, I would pick up the ball and we would play catch. This afternoon, I don't feel much like doing anything. I just want to keep my distance from Loren. Junior gets mad at me because I don't want to play catch, calling me a baby.

I yell, "Shut up!"

He then calls me, "Four eyes."

I get mad and tell him, "Leave me alone."

Loren picks up the ball and begins to play catch with Junior. I sit on the stairs, watching them both and wondering to myself, "Why? Why me?"

I hear a car pull in the driveway. It must be dad. I glance at Loren.

He looks at me and says, "Don't say anything."

I don't look up at him, but down at the ground and say, "I won't."

I see dad walking across the grass.

I go running towards him and say, "Dad, dad, I missed you."

He picks me up in his strong arms, gives me a hug and kiss, and lets me know he missed me, too. I don't usually go running to dad, when he gets home from work, but today is different. I really need to feel his arms wrapped around me.

Loren stays at the house long enough for dad to pay him.

As he is leaving, he looks at me and says to dad, "The kids were great, and they didn't get into any trouble. If you need me to watch them again, just let me know."

My stomach turns. How could he stand there, talk to dad and act like it was such a great day. Sure it probably was for him, but it certainly wasn't for me.

Loren never did watch us again. I never told dad what he did to me. Actually, I didn't tell dad, because I thought he would get mad at me. I would live with yet another secret tucked away inside of me until adulthood.

Chapter Six
Two Encounters

October 1961 through October 1965 would bring me two encounters with the Mayor of the small town we lived in. The first would be a direct encounter during the spring of 1962. The second would be an indirect one, during the autumn of 1965.

It's the spring of 1962. Remember Dave and Linda, the friends that live next door. Well, today, we, The Four Musketeers, decide to venture to the farm, which the Mayor owns, to tease the bulls. We've been warned not to go to there, but we do it anyway.

Once we reach the farm, we climb under the wooden fence. I walk towards the bulls and yell to them to get their attention. Before I know it, they start running towards me. I can feel the ground shake. I become excited and scared at the same time. I turn and run towards the fence for safety. I'm running so fast that I gasp for breath. Once I reach the safety of the fence, I catch a little more air, turn towards the bulls, laugh and say, "Ha, ha, you didn't get me."

I hear a deep stern voice. Out of nowhere the Mayor appears.

I turn, look up and hear him say, "You children should not be teasing the bulls."

The four of us tremble in silence. I don't know what to say. The few minutes standing there feels like hours.

The silence is broken, when the Mayor speaks. He looks at each of us and says, "If you ever do this again, I will speak to your parents."

No one says a word. A few minutes pass.

Looking down at the ground, I speak up, "I promise we will never tease the bulls again."

He says, "Now, go home."

With our heads down, we turn and walk away. As we get closer to the house, Dave breaks the silence, "The next time we won't get caught."

I turn, look at him and say, "We made a promise."

The four of us continue our walk home. No words are spoken. Silence fills the air.

This particular Saturday morning in July of 1965 would be unlike all the others. A typical morning would consist of a leisurely breakfast of bacon, eggs, toast and chocolate milk. Then, the three of us would hang out for a couple hours, watching cartoons. There would be no hustle and bustle like other mornings. Instead, it would be very laid back. Today would be different.

I hear voices coming from the living room. I listen. It sounds like someone is crying. I wonder what's going on. I walk out of my bedroom, down the hall, through the kitchen and into the living room. I see dad on the couch. He's holding someone. I wonder who she is. She has a sheet wrapped around her, and she is crying.

Dad sees me standing in the doorway and says, "Go back to bed."

I look at him and say, "I am hungry."

He says, "Go to your room and play."

As I walk back to my room, I think to myself, "Go to my room and play? I never just play in my room."

Once there, I sit on the bed. I listen to hear what is being said in the other room. They're talking too low. I'm not able to hear them. A few minutes pass. I hear the sound of footsteps coming from the hall. I hear dad's voice. I turn my head and see her go into the bathroom.

Dad looks at me and says, "I have to leave for a little while. I want you to make no noise and watch your brother until I get back."

I see her come out of the bathroom. She has long brown hair.

Dad puts his arm around her, as they walk down the hall. I hear the kitchen door open. They must be leaving. I stand at my bedroom window, watching for the car to pull out of the driveway. I see them. Dad makes a right turn out of the driveway and goes up the road. I wonder where he is going. I wonder who she is. I wonder why she is crying.

I turn from the window, walk out into the hall, through the kitchen and into the living room. I look out the front window. I'm not looking for dad. I'm looking for the horses across the road. I don't see them. I need to talk with them. I've not been in the house alone until now. I hope Junior doesn't wake up. What will I say to him, if he wakes up, before dad gets back?

I see dad's car coming down the road. It doesn't look like she's in it. He pulls in the driveway. I sit on the couch, waiting for him and wondering what he will say. I hear his footsteps on the stairs. The kitchen door opens, and he walks into the living room.

He asks, "Is Junior awake?"

I say, "No. Where did you go?"

He says, "I took Ernestine home."

I ask, "Why was she crying?"

He says, "We did grown up things."

I ask, "What kind of grown up things?"

He says, "We did things you and I can't do."

46

I ask, "Why was she sad?"

He says, "She's no longer a virgin."

I ask, "What's a virgin?"

He says, "One day you will find out."

Junior is awake. He walks into the living room and says, "I'm hungry."

Dad says, "Let's fix breakfast."

After breakfast, instead of going to the living room to sit in front of the television to watch cartoons, I retreat to my room. After getting dressed, I sit on my bed and think about what dad said about Ernestine. I wonder if she had to put his penis in her mouth. I wonder if she liked the taste. I wonder if she will be back. If she comes back, maybe I won't have to put it in my mouth, and maybe I won't have to taste that awful stuff.

It's a Saturday morning just a few short months after Ernestine was at the house. Dad has not mentioned her name, and I've not awakened in the morning to find her in the living room.

After breakfast, dad tells both Junior and I, "We will be moving in a couple of weeks."

Junior looks at me, and I look at him. I think to myself, "I don't want to move."

I look at dad and say, "I don't want to move."

Dad says, "We have to."

I ask, "Why?"

He says, "Because, we have to."

I ask, "Where are we going to move?"

He says, "We are going to the city."

I say, "I will miss Linda, Dave and all my friends at school."

He says, "You'll make new friends."

I tell him again, "I don't want to move!"

He looks at me and says, "I am the boss in this house, and you will do what you are told to do."

I sit at the table for a few minutes. I don't say a word. I want to scream. I want to cry. I don't want to move. I have to get out of the house.

I look at him and say, "I'm going outside."

He says, "Okay."

I stand in the backyard and listen to the sound of the birds chirping. I look up at the tree and see a bird sitting on a branch.

I ask it, "Please take me away."

The bird flies off, leaving me behind.

I feel sad. I'm mad. I look up into the sky and ask God, "Why do we have to move?"

As I'm standing in the backyard, I hear the door open that leads to our apartment. Out of the corner of my eye, I see dad walking down the stairs with a cup of coffee in his hand. He sits, lights a cigarette and calls me over. I hear him calling, but pretend I don't hear. He calls me again.

I turn and look at him.

Dad says, "Come here, my little girl."

I walk over to the stairs, crying, "I don't want to move."

He says, "Come here."

I go to him, and he holds me in his arms.

I ask, "Why do we have to move?"

He says, "I got into trouble."

I ask, "What kind of trouble? "

He tells me, "The Mayor said we have to leave."

I ask, "Why?"

He says, "Remember the morning Ernestine was here?"

Without hesitation I answer, "Yes. How could I forget?"

He says, "Because she is no longer a virgin, we have to leave."

I say, "Who cares what the Mayor says?"

Dad says, "If we don't leave, both you and Junior will be taken away."

I ask, "What do you mean?"

He says, "If they take you away, you will never see me again."

I start to cry. "I don't want to be taken away."

He holds me in his arms and tells me, "I love you. No one will take you away."

It's October of 1965. It's moving day. The truck and car are all loaded with all our belongings. Dave and Linda come to say good bye. I look at Linda, trying to hold back the tears, but I can't. I start to cry.

Junior calls me, a "baby."

Linda starts to cry.

He calls us both, "Big babies."

I reach for Linda. We embrace one another. God, I don't want to let go of her, and I don't want to have to say good bye.

Dad says, "Come on. We've got to go."

I squeeze her one last time, look into her eyes and say, "Good bye."

I turn to dad and ask, "Can I say good bye to the horses?"

He says, "Yes."

I run across the road and down to the fence. They see me coming and run towards me. They look just as happy to see me, as I am to see them. If I had one wish that could be granted, I would wish I could become a horse this very moment. I wouldn't have to move, and I would forever be with my trusted friends. But I know this is not the case. I look at each of them one more time. I let them know they have been the best friends anyone could have. I start to cry. I pat each one of them on the head and say, " Good bye."

I walk away. I don't look back.

The Mayor of the little town we lived in would forever remain a part of my memory. I didn't know at the age of seven how powerful a person he was. I just knew it was wrong to go to his farm and tease the bulls. I would realize at the age of eleven just how powerful he was. He made a decision as the Mayor of the little town we lived in to protect his daughter from further harm. It was a wise and noble decision. Once again, we had to move, because of unwise decisions dad made at the cost of others.

Chapter Seven
A Day to Remember

In October 1965 the move, from the country to the city slums in Syracuse, New York, bring with it change and awareness. I hadn't realized, until we moved that we weren't by any means well off. The apartment and neighborhood we live in didn't bring with it the serene, secure feeling I felt, when we lived in the country. The adjustment to school would be unbearable at times. I would learn the meaning and consequences of using the word " Nigger." The biggest change would come with Dad's newfound friend. She would not only become his friend, but also a part of our family.

The apartment we live in is on the second floor above a store. The outside of the building isn't much to look at. When you stand in front of the building, all you see are SALE SIGNS for food and sandwiches. It isn't very colorful; it looks dirty and run down. I knew from the first day I wasn't going to like living here.

The apartment is small, dark, and there aren't very many windows. Dad and Junior share a bedroom. I have my own room. For me, having my own bedroom is the only highlight of the apartment. The first morning waking up and going into the bathroom would be a rude awakening for me. I stand at the sink, brushing my teeth and notice these bugs crawling around. I let out a big scream. Dad comes running.

He asks, "What is wrong?"

I show him the bugs near the bathroom sink and the ones crawling up the wall. He hits them with his shoe, smashing them on the wall. The ones he is not able to get go running to safety. They're brown, big and ugly. I've not seen bugs like this before.

I ask him, "What kind of bugs are they?"

He says, "They are cockroaches."

I say sarcastically, "I don't like these bugs. I don't like the apartment."

He says nothing.

I go to my room to get dressed and think to myself, "Why do we have to live here?"

Kathy lives in the apartment across the hall from us with her son Joey. It seems dad has taken a liking to her. She doesn't work and is home most of the time. She's pretty, has long hair and doesn't pass up an opportunity to make herself available. Dad has to leave for work, before we go to school, so Kathy keeps an eye on us. Although she is supposed to be watching out for us, she doesn't get up in the morning. Instead, she leaves the door to her apartment open, so she can listen for us. I could never figure out how she was able to listen for us, if she was sleeping. Dad gets me up just before he leaves for work. My morning routine and responsibilities during the week consist of getting Junior up, fixing us both cereal, then making sure we both get to school on time. It is rare for us to have any contact with Kathy in the morning.

Shortly after the move, dad begins to spend most of the evening hours with Kathy in her apartment, rather than with us. This takes some adjusting for me. I'm use to having him home in the evening. A typical evening during the week would consist of dinner, a bath, and sitting watching a television program with him, then off to bed. Now right after dinner, he rushes over to her apartment. Both doors are kept open. Instead of sitting on the couch next to Dad watching television, I find myself straining to hear what they are talking about. Often times, I hear them laughing and wonder what could be so funny.

Though he spends a good part of his evening at her apartment, he always comes to tuck me in. The hug, kiss on my forehead and the words, "I love you " remains the same. Thank God, this doesn't change!

Dad has stopped coming to my room every night. Instead, he only comes a couple times a week. I welcome this change. I think he might be sleeping at Kathy's most nights, but I'm not sure. Most times, when he comes to my room and I have my hand around his penis and I'm shaking it, my hand gets so tired and feels numb. Often times, my arm and hand don't feel like they're attached to the rest of my body. On those nights that he doesn't come to my room, I thank God I haven't had to shake or put it in my mouth.

I've only gone to the new school for about a month and have decided I don't like it. The kids are so mean to one another. Today, I hear a classmate call another classmate a "Nigger." The boy, who was called the name, ran after the other boy. They fight. The other kids stand around, laughing and shouting, "Get him. Beat the Nigger up." I get scared. I've not heard the word "Nigger" before.

During dinner I ask Dad, "What does the word "Nigger" mean?"

He looks at me and says nothing.

A few minutes pass, and he asks, "Where did you hear that word?"

I say, "I was on the playground today at school, and one of the boys called another boy this name. They began to fight."

Dad says, "It's not a nice word."

I ask, "Why?"

He says, "White people call Black people this name."

I let Dad know, "I don't understand what you mean."

He says in a stern voice, "Don't use that word."

I've gotten the message loud and clear not to say it, but I still don't understand why.

I look at him and say, "I won't."

Junior speaks up and says, "They call Black people this name all the time."

Dad looks at him and says in a harsh voice, "Never call someone a Nigger."

The school scene has not improved. Just a few days after Dad made it very clear not to use the word "Nigger," I find myself protecting and defending Junior. We're walking home from school. I hear the words, "That's him." The next thing I know a boy is pushing Junior.

Junior says, "Cathy, get him."

I look at the boy and say, "Leave my brother alone."

He says, "Who are you?"

I look at him and say, "I'm his sister."

He looks at me and says, "I'm going to beat his ass for calling my brother a Nigger."

I turn, look at Junior, and he says, "I didn't say anything to him."

The boy pushes Junior again.

I say, "Leave him alone," as I position myself in front of Junior.

He yells, "Get out of my way!"

I shout, "No!"

He tries to push me out of the way. I get mad and push him back. He punches me in the arm. I punch him back. He grabs my hair and pulls me down on the ground.

I get real mad. I'm able to get on top of him and pin him down.

I look at him and yell, "Leave my brother alone!"

He says nothing.

I say, "If you touch my brother again, I will hurt you!"

I get up, noticing there are a lot of kids standing around us.

I look at Junior and say, "Let's go home."

As we are walking away, I hear voices say, "He is a trouble maker."

There were many days that followed when I would have to beat up kids, because of names Junior would call them. At first, it would only be one kid. A short time after this first incident, a gang of kids would run after him on a regular basis, right after school was dismissed. I didn't have a problem with having to beat up one kid at a time, but I wasn't able to beat up a gang of them.

So we came up with a plan. As soon as the dismissal bell would ring, I would bolt out of school. Junior would do the same. We would meet at the fence in front of the school. This usually allowed us enough time to walk home, rather than having to run.

Today, the plan didn't work. I hear voices. I turn my head and see the gang is a short distance behind us.

I hear someone yell, "Get them."

I get scared not knowing what to do.

Junior says, "Let's go through the backyards." He starts running.

I follow a short distance behind. We're in this backyard. The only way to get out is to climb the fence. I don't know what to do.

Junior says, "Come on." He starts climbing the fence.

I say, "The fence is too high."

He says, "Come on, or they will get you."

I can feel my heart pumping and know I must climb the fence. I reach for the top of the fence. I pull myself up. My skirt gets caught on a nail.

I yell out for Junior to help.

He says, "Hurry up."

I tell him, "My skirt is caught."

He says, "Pull it."

I pull it and manage to yank myself over the fence. I stand on the ground, trying to catch my breath.

Junior says, "Let's go."

I say, "I'm coming."

We run through yet another backyard and onto a sidewalk. I don't hear the voices.

Junior says, "They aren't chasing us. We outsmarted them."

As I stand trying to catch my breath, I look at him and say sternly, "You're a troublemaker. You can't call other kids names."

It's a relief to finally reach the apartment. As we climb the stairs, I think to myself, "God, I hate that school."

Kathy's apartment door is open, as it always is. She usually just yells and says, "Hi." Today is unlike other days. She is standing in her apartment doorway.

She looks at both of us and says, "You two look like you've been running."

I say nothing.

Junior blurts out, "Yeah, those kids were chasing us."

Kathy says, "If you don't tell your father, I'll let you skip school tomorrow."

This sounds good to me. I'm getting pretty tired of having to run home.

Junior is pleased and says, "Really."

Kathy says, "Yes, remember not a word to your father."

He looks at me with doubt in his eyes and says, "As long as Cathy doesn't tell Dad."

I look at him and say, "I don't want to go to that stupid school. I won't say anything."

Later that evening after Dad has tucked me in bed, given me a hug and kissed me good night, I lay in my bed formulating a plan. We can use our lunch money to buy soda and candy at the store, then go to the park to play. We won't have to run through anyone's backyard or climb any fences to get home. Kathy told us she wouldn't tell dad. Junior won't say anything. I'm excited and can't wait for morning to come.

The next morning dad gets me up and as usual says, "I'll see you later."

I murmur, "Have a nice day."

Out the door and off to work he goes.

Both apartment doors are open. I listen for any sounds coming from Kathy's apartment. It's quiet. She's probably still sleeping.

I don't rush to get Junior up. After all, we're not going to school. I make my way to the bathroom to brush my teeth. While reaching for my toothbrush (damn), I see a cockroach. I'm so sick of those things. I no longer scream, when I see one. Instead, I reach for the newspaper on the back of the toilet. Most times I'm able to kill it, before it runs to safety. Ah, it didn't get away. I hate the cockroaches. I hate this apartment. I wish we could move back to the country.

I walk into Junior's room. He asks, "Is dad gone?"

I say, "He's gone to work."

Junior asks, "Are we going to school?"

I say, "No. Get up and get dressed, so we can leave."

I make my way to the kitchen, grab some bowls from the cupboard, fill them with cereal, and then milk. As I sit at the table, waiting for him, I think, "For someone, who didn't want to go to school, he sure is moving slow."

He finally makes his way to the kitchen and says, "I'm hungry."

I look at him and say, "Eat, so we can leave."

A few minutes pass.

Junior says, "We are going to have fun today."

I look at him and say, "What if dad finds out? "

He says, "He won't."

I say, "If he does, we are going to be in big trouble."

He says with leeriness in his voice, "He'll only find out, if you tell him."

I say, "I'm not going to tell. I don't want to get into trouble."

We finish breakfast. I grab the lunch money Dad has left for us. I walk to my book bag and realize I won't need it today. We aren't going to school.

The sun is shining. The street is quiet. Although, there is a chill in the air, it doesn't bother me. I'm just happy to be free from school.

Junior says, "Let's go to the park."

I say with hesitation in my voice, "What if someone sees us?"

He says, "No one will see us. Everyone is at school."

As we're walking down the street to the park, I say, "I don't like our new school. I think the kids are mean. Why do you call kids names?"

He laughs and says, "I don't like them."

I say, "I can beat up one kid at a time for you, but not six at the same time."

Again, he laughs.

I think to myself, "I wish he would just keep his mouth shut."

We walk the rest of the way to the park in silence. It is quiet and empty. Today, there is no need to wait for someone to get off a swing. We have the park all to ourselves. We both take full advantage of this.

After swinging, I turn to Junior and tell him, "I don't like Kathy."

He looks at me and asks, "Why?"

I say, "She never spends time with us, and dad's always in her apartment."

He says, "Yeah, dad goes over there, after we've gone to bed."

I say, "What do you mean? "

He tells me Dad waits until we go to sleep, then goes back over to Kathy's apartment. He says, " Sometimes he sleeps there."

I say, "How do you know! "

He says, "Sometimes I wake up at night, and he isn't in his bed."

I think to myself, "Maybe, this is why he no longer comes to my room every night."

Junior says, "I think he likes her."

I sit in silence for a few minutes and wonder if Junior likes her. I sure hope not. I turn to him and ask, "Do you like her?"

He says without hesitation, "No."

I ask, " Why? "

He doesn't give me an answer.

A few minutes pass, and he says, "Let's go to the store."

As we walk to the store, I think about Kathy. She's pretty. Dad seems to like her. She doesn't say much to me. She knows we're skipping school and said she wouldn't tell. I guess that maybe she's okay. We're at the store. Junior heads right for the candy.

The owner of the store asks, "Why aren't you kids in school?"

I stand next to the counter, not knowing what to say.

Junior looks at the owner and blurts out, "We're skipping school."

The owner says, "You kids are going to get into trouble."

I look at Junior and say, "Shut up and get your candy."

He grabs a couple candy bars. I'm becoming very impatient.

I look at the owner and ask, "How much?"

He says, "You kids should be in school."

I ask him again, "How much?"

He tells me the amount.

I nervously pull the money from my pocket. God, I just want to run out of the store. I give him the money we owe; we both turn and walk out of the store. Once we hit the sidewalk, we run down the street and head for the park. As we sit there, enjoying our candy bars, I hear the school bell. It's lunchtime.

I look at Junior and say, "We should leave the park."

He says, "I'm hungry."

I say, "Let's go home and fix lunch."

As we walk up the stairs, I hear music. Kathy's door is open.

I turn to look at Junior and say, "Be quiet." I don't want her to know we're home. I reach in my pocket for the key to unlock the door. As both Junior and I are walking into the apartment, I hear a voice. I turn my head and notice Kathy standing in her doorway. Damn, I didn't want her to know we were home.

She says, "You didn't go to school?"

Junior speaks up and says, "No. We skipped."

She says, "I know. The school called me, after they called your father at work."

Oh, no. We're in trouble. My hands feel sweaty. My stomach begins to tighten up. Dad knows we didn't go to school.

Junior says, "We'll tell him you said it was okay for us to skip school."

Kathy stands in her doorway with her arms crossed and says, "When I spoke with your father, he sounded mad. By the way, I didn't tell you to skip school."

I stand in silence. I can't believe she isn't going to tell Dad she is the one, who suggested it.

Junior says, "You told us we could skip school, as long as we didn't tell dad."

She says, "That was before he found out."

Junior looks at her and says, "You lied to us!"

She laughs and says, "You two are the ones, who are in trouble."

I look at her in disgust and tell Junior, "Let's go fix lunch."

We walk into the apartment. I don't close the door gently, but slam it.

I hear her say, "Your father wants you to stay in the apartment the rest of the day."

As I walk to the kitchen, I think, "I don't like her. She lies. She thinks its funny we're in trouble. She blew it! No more chances."

I'm sitting on the couch and hear footsteps coming up the stairs. I know its dad. I hear two voices.

Junior stares at me.

I look at him and say, "We shouldn't have skipped school."

The door opens. Dad walks in.

God, I feel sick to my stomach.

He looks at both of us, raises his voice and says, "You two just can't behave. You have to get into trouble."

I don't like it, when Dad raises his voice. It scares me.

Junior says, "Kathy told us we could skip school."

I say, "I don't like the school. The kids are mean. I'm tired of having to run home, because they want to beat up Junior. I want to move back to the country!"

Junior says, "Kathy is a trouble maker and lied to us."

Dad raises his voice even more.

I start to cry.

He yells, "Cathy, you're suppose to take care of your brother."

I look at him and say, "I did!"

Dad tells us both, "Go to your rooms until dinner!"

I sit on my bed in my room, feeling bad. I know it was wrong not to go to school, but it was also wrong of Kathy to lie to us. If she had never mentioned it yesterday, we would have never done it. If we hadn't, we wouldn't be in trouble, and dad wouldn't be upset.

Dad yells for us to come to dinner.

I'm consumed with thoughts and feelings about the day. I'm not very hungry and find myself picking at my food.

Junior, on the other hand, eats like there is no tomor-row.

After dinner dad says, "You both get ready for bed, no television and no snack."

Junior says, "It wasn't our fault!"

Dad says, "I don't want to hear it!"

Junior never seems to know, when to keep his mouth shut.

He looks at dad and says, "I don't like her. She's a trouble maker."

Although I agree with him, I know better than to say anything. After all, it was wrong of us to skip school.

Dad says, "It doesn't matter what you like. I am the boss. Now, both of you get your pajamas on and get to bed!"

I walk slowly to my room. I can hear dad in the kitchen washing the dishes. After crawling into bed, I lay there wondering, if Dad will come to my room tonight. I hope he does. I want to tell him I'm sorry for skipping school. I want to tell him I don't like Kathy. I lay in my bed, staring at the ceiling for what seems to be hours, waiting for him to come to my room. I awaken in the morning and feel disappointed. Dad didn't come to my room.

Dad tells us, "I am taking you to school this morning. Directly to the principal's office."

I can feel the muscles in my stomach begin to tighten. Oh no, now I have to face the principal. I don't move as quickly this morning. The knot in my stomach tightens.

Dad says, "Hurry up! I bet you two will never skip school again."

I think to myself, "He's right. I won't skip school again."

We walk into the school.

63

I hear some kids say, "There is the trouble maker." It's obvious they're referring to Junior. I ignore their comments and follow a short distance behind Dad.

We enter the principal's office. Both he and Dad greet one another with a handshake. I've not been in his office before. I feel sick to my stomach.

Dad says, while taking his belt off, "These two will not skip school again. If they do, I will use this." He holds the belt up in the air, so we can see it.

God, I've never gotten hit with that. It looks like it would hurt.

The principal says, "You must talk to your son and tell him not to call the other kids names."

Dad looks at Junior and says, "You will keep your mouth shut, or you will get a taste of this."

I think to myself, "Maybe now, he will keep his mouth shut."

The principal looks at Dad and says, "I am glad you came to the school. Obviously, you care for your children."

Dad looks at him and says, "If you have any more problems, call me at work."

The principal assures him, "I will."

Later the same day as we are walking up the stairs after school to the apartment, I hear Kathy's voice. I ignore her. I don't want to see her. I don't want to talk to her. As I'm entering the apartment, I look in her direction.

She says with a smile on her face, "You went to school today."

How dare she stand there with a smile on her face; she thinks it's a big joke. Because of her, we got into trouble.

Junior says, "You trouble maker. We don't like you."

She brags, "I am going to be your new mommy."

We're both dumbfounded. I can't believe what I've just heard. There's no way she is going to replace my mom.

I say, "My mother is dead, and you aren't going to be my mother!"

She says, "Oh, yes I am."

Junior says, "Go away. We don't like you."

I start to cry. I say to Junior, "I want mom!"

She says, "I will be your mother."

I say, "You lied and got us into trouble."

I turn, walk into the apartment and slam the door. I'll be damned, if she becomes my mother!

I turn look at Junior and say, "I want mom back." I can't control my crying. I feel the warmth of tears rolling down my cheeks.

Junior demands, "Stop being a baby."

I say, "But, I miss mom."

He says, "You always start crying, whenever anyone mentions her name."

I turn to him and say, "You don't understand. You don't remember her, but I do. I miss her."

A few hours have passed. I'm sitting on the couch waiting for Dad to get home. I hear his footsteps coming up the stairs.

He opens the door.

I waste no time. I look at him and say, "Kathy told us she is going to be our mother."

He just stands there, not saying a word.

I feel the build up of tears. I can't and don't hold them back. I begin to cry.

Dad walks towards me.

I look up at him and ask, "Is it true?"

He looks at me and says, "Yes."

65

I say, "My mom is dead. I want my mom, and no one else! I don't like Kathy. She lied and got us into trouble. She never spends any time with us, just you."

He says, "Now, she will be able to spend time with you."

I say, "I'll never call her mom."

He says, "You don't have to."

I say, "I won't!"

Dad calls Junior into the front room and tells us both, "We will be moving soon."

No, not another move. I'm getting tired of this.

Junior says, "Where?"

Dad says, "To a better neighborhood."

Junior asks, "Is she and her son coming with us?"

Dad says, "Yes."

Junior says, "I don't want her to."

Dad says, "Both you and Cathy will do, as I tell you to do! You need someone to take care of you."

Junior says, "Not her!"

Dad says, "Shut up!"

Tonight, dad comes to my room and holds me in his arms. I start to cry. "I don't like Kathy. I don't want her to be my mother."

He says, "I love Kathy."

I say, "I don't love her. I love you."

He asks, "Do you want me to be happy?"

I say, "Yes."

He says, "I want her to live with us. We'll live in a bigger apartment. There won't be any cockroaches. You'll have your own room, and we will still do things to one another.

I look at Dad and ask, "Do you love me?"

He says, "Yes. You will always be my special little girl."

His arms feel so strong wrapped around me. The warmth of his skin feels good next to mine. I think, "Dad still loves me, even though I skipped school.

He tells me, "You will always be my special little girl."

I want Dad to be happy. I will do, as he asks.

Chapter Eight

Fear

The unraveling, of the weeks and months that followed the move, would bring with it fear and jealousy. Home would no longer be a safe haven. School becomes my great escape.

We live on the third floor of a three-story apartment building. Although the building doesn't have an elevator, I don't mind, having to climb the many stairs to our apartment. Junior and Joey share a bedroom, I get my own room; Dad and Kathy have their bedroom. I begin to realize it isn't so bad being the oldest and only girl. Junior has to share his room, and I get my own.

In March of 1966, we've lived in the apartment for about five months. The kids at this school don't seem as mean. I don't have to beat kids up for Junior, and I walk home from school instead of running.

I've taken a liking to my teacher, Mrs. Schaefer. She is an older lady, heavyset and tends to smile a lot. No one seems to smile at home, so this is a treat for me. Before leaving the classroom each day, she tells me she will see me in the morning. I notice she doesn't tell the other kids she will see them in the morning. I FEEL SPECIAL.

Sometimes when I'm walking home from school, I think about her. I imagine I am going home with her and think to myself, "She doesn't yell. She smiles. And, I bet, she would be nice to me."

As I continue the walk home, reality sinks in. I begin to think about what I will need to do once I'm home. Kathy has taught me how to perk coffee in the coffeepot. It has become my chore to make sure a fresh pot of coffee is made, before Dad gets home. I don't mind, though, after all it is for Dad. After making coffee, I usually have to peel lots of potatoes for dinner. This is a tedious chore for me. Sometimes, she'll sit watching me. This always makes me nervous. Instead of paying attention to what I am doing, I begin to cut the potato skin too thick.

She notices, yells, and tells me I am wasting food. Junior and I are responsible for cleaning up the kitchen after dinner. I enjoy this time he and I are able to spend together. It's the only time we're together other than walking to and from school. It is a time for us to talk, pick on one another and share our feelings about Kathy.

Tonight, he tells me he doesn't like her. Saying, "She is always yelling at me for no reason. You should talk to Dad. He'll listen to you."

I look at him and whisper; "Dad won't listen. He let her move in. He cares more about her than us."

Tonight, I lay in my bed and wonder if Dad will come to see me. The pattern since we've moved has been, he comes to my room every other night, once Kathy is in the tub, with a paper towel in hand. Sure enough, I hear the tub water running in the bathroom. I see a shadow on the wall.

He walks into my room and stands next to the bed, saying, "Come on hurry up. We don't have much time."

I sit up, grab his penis and begin to shake it. I just want to break the ugly thing in half. I'm tired of having to do this all the time.

Dad says, "Come on. Shake it faster!"

I continue to shake it. Without realizing it, I begin to squeeze it as hard as I can.

Dad says, "Not so hard."

I let up on my tight squeeze, continue to shake it and say, "I'm sorry." My hand and arm become numb, as I continue.

Dad's breathing becomes deeper and louder. The awful stuff comes out of his penis. He hands me the paper towel.

I wipe his penis off, then my hand. As he is putting his penis back into his pants, I look up at him and say, "Junior and I don't like Kathy. We don't want her to live with us." He says, "She is staying. I need her to watch you."

I tell him, "She yells all the time and is mean to us."

He bends down, wraps his arms around me and tells me. "I love you."

I tell him. "I love you too."

Dad says, "Goodnight," and walks out of the room.

I lay awake in my bed for a long time tonight, thinking about dad. I wonder why he won't tell her to leave? It has to be more than her just watching us. I wonder if he loves her more than me?

Since the move, we no longer have the luxury of staying at school to eat lunch.

Dad tells us he can't afford it. Actually, he could if she and her son weren't living with us. Instead, we make the daily walk home then return to school. Lunch at home is physically filling, but by no means filling in any other way.

I usually walk into the apartment only to find Kathy sitting in front of the television, watching a game show or some stupid soap opera. She doesn't get off the couch to fix or have lunch with us; instead she tells me to fix Joey a sandwich and to clean up the mess, before going back to school.

Today, as Junior and I walk back to school, he tells me he heard Dad and Kathy talking about a baby.

He says, "Kathy is going to have a baby."

I turn to him and say, "No."

He says, "Look how fat she is getting."

I say, "No way. I'll ask Dad."

He says, "If she is going to have a baby, you know she will never leave."

As we continue to walk to school, I remember back to the time after the incident with Ernestine and Dad. I remember Dad telling me they did grown up things. I remember thinking to myself then, "When I get older, Dad and I can do grown up things and have a baby." The thought of Kathy having a baby preoccupies my thoughts all afternoon. I can't wait to get home to ask Dad, if it is true.

Dad walks into the kitchen. My eyes meet his. I look at him and ask, "Is it true?"

He asks, "Is what true?"

I say, "That she is going to have a baby."

He has a surprised look on his face. He stands there. A few minutes pass.

I ask again, "Is she?"

He looks at me and says, "Yes."

I can't believe what my ears have just heard. How could he let this happen? I'm suppose to be his "special little girl." I can feel my eyes filling with water. I want to cry. Instead, I resist.

Junior walks into the kitchen; I look at him and say, "You were right."

He says, "She is going to have a baby?"

Dad says, "Yes."

Kathy walks into the kitchen and demands to know what we were talking about.

Dad looks at her and says, "They know you're pregnant."

71

She says, "Good, I told you two I was going to be your mother."

I feel tears rolling down my cheeks. I look at Junior, Dad, then Kathy and say, " I don't want you to be my mother! My mother is dead. I will never call you mom! " I can't stop crying. I look at Dad and say, "I want my mom!"

He says, " Stop it, or go to your room!"

I waste no time, exiting the kitchen. Once I'm in my room, I slam the door and throw myself on the bed. I can't believe she is going to have a baby! She can't take care of Joey. She treats me like a slave and makes me do EVERYTHING around the house.

She yells, screams and is so mean to us. How can this be true? I don't want her to stay!

But, I don't have a choice. Dad has always told me I'm his special little girl. Why then is he is letting her stay? I don't understand. I bury my head in my pillow. I don't want anyone to hear me cry.

It's June 19, 1966. Dad comes to my room tonight. It's Father's Day, and tomorrow is my birthday.

He whispers in my ear and says, "You are my special little girl and I love you."

I look at him and say, "Happy Father's Day, Dad. You're the best."

He pulls his penis out of his pants and says, "I have a present for you."

I hear the word present and wonder what it could be. Then I realize he's talking about his penis.

He says, "I want you to put it in your mouth."

Oh God, here we go again. I don't want to put that smelly awful thing in my mouth. I reach for it.

Dad moves closer.

I put it in my mouth. It smells and taste awful.

Dad says, "Shake it."

I squeeze and shake it at the same time. I wish I could just bite the damn thing off.

Dad has his hands on the back of my head. The stuff comes out of his penis.

I try to pull my head away.

He forces my head forward.

I can't get my mouth off of it. I want so much to spit the stuff out of my mouth, but instead I swallow.

Dad pulls it out of my mouth, bends down and tells me, "I love you."

I say, "I love you too."

He tells me, "Kathy will be going into the hospital soon to have the baby."

I ask, "How long will she be there?"

He says, "For a few days."

I say, "Good. I need a break from her."

Dad says, "We will be able to spend time with one another."

I think to myself, "Oh no, does this mean I'll have to put it in my mouth every night."

He turns to me says, "Goodnight," and walks out of the room.

I lay in bed, not liking the taste I have in my mouth. I want to get up to brush my teeth, but I don't. I'm supposed to be sleeping. If I get up to go to the bathroom, Kathy might yell at me for being awake. The last thing I want is for her to yell at me.

It's June 20, 1966, my birthday. I turn twelve today. I'm excited about going to school. Mrs. Schaefer always brings cupcakes, when it is someone's birthday. We usually sing happy birthday and have cupcakes in the afternoon. I hope she doesn't forget my birthday today.

On the way to school Junior says, "I wonder, if she will make a cake for you?"

I say, "I don't know and don't really care if she does."

He says, " I know dad will bring a cake home."

I say, "I hope so."

Mrs. Schaefer greets me, as I am walking into the classroom and says, " Good morning and happy birthday."

I don't know what to say. I look at her and smile. As I walk to my desk, I think, "Mrs. Schaefer is so nice. I wonder if she brought cupcakes in for me? I hope so."

It's almost time for the bell to ring for lunch. She announces this afternoon we will have cupcakes to celebrate my birthday.

I'm embarrassed and don't know what to say. I look up at her, smile and think to myself, "This is the nicest thing anyone has done for me."

The lunch bell rings. As I make my way to the front of the room and walk towards the door, Mrs. Schaefer says, "Cathy have a nice lunch, and I'll see you in a little while."

I look up at her, smile and say, "Okay."

As we are walking home, I turn, look at Junior and say, "I hope she is in a good mood. I don't want to hear her yell."

He says, " Maybe, she will be nice. It is your birthday."

I say, "I hope so."

As we enter the apartment through the kitchen, Joey sees us and comes running.

Kathy as usual is sitting on the couch, watching television.

I wonder if she ever gets up off her butt during the day. Before I get a chance to take my jacket off, Kathy yells out, "Fix Joey some lunch."

As the three of us sit at the table, eating our peanut butter and jelly sandwich, Kathy walks into the kitchen.

I think to myself, "Oh no, here we go. I must be in trouble."

She looks at both Junior and I and says, "I have a lot of chores that need to be done today. So, rest up."

I don't say a word. I know better.

She doesn't bother to tell us to have a nice afternoon. She doesn't even acknowledge that it's my birthday.

Thank God, its time to go back to school.

Mrs. Schaefer announces she has to leave the classroom for a few minutes. She tells us, "Sit quietly." She leaves the room.

I sit, wondering where she has gone.

A few minutes later, she enters the room. She's carries a box in her arms and places it on her desk.

I wonder what could be in the box.

She turns, looks at me and says to everyone, " We have a birthday to celebrate."

I feel tightness in my stomach. My face feels warm. I'm embarrassed.

She says, "Today is Cathy's birthday. Let's sing."

All my classmates sing.

I can feel my eyes filling with water. I fight back the tears. I want to cry, because I'm happy, not because I'm sad.

Mrs. Schaefer says, "Cathy, come help me pass out the cupcakes."

They look so good, vanilla frosting with sprinkles.

After everyone gets one, she looks at me and says, "We saved the best for last."

The frosting is sweet and yummy. The cupcake is chocolate inside, my favorite. I wonder if she knew this.

The dismissal bell rings. As my classmates are leaving the room, they say to me, "Happy Birthday."

I feel good. I feel happy.

As I leave the classroom, Mrs. Schaefer looks at me and says, " Happy Birthday, Cathy. You are so special."

I look up at her, smile and say, " Thank you." I want so much for her to hold me. I want her to take me home. My thoughts drift to Kathy. God, I hope she's in a good mood.

As we begin climbing the stairs to the apartment, I feel my stomach muscles tighten. Today is my birthday, a time of celebration, but I don't feel much like celebrating. Before entering the apartment, I take a deep breath. I hope, she's in a good mood. As I walk through the kitchen, I notice there are dishes in the sink. Bet she didn't get up off her lazy butt all day. It smells like something has been baked. I scan the counter top and table to look for a cake. I don't see one. How stupid of me to think she would bake a cake for my birthday.

As I walk through the living room headed to my bedroom to change my clothes, she looks at me and says, "Don't just stand there. Go make some coffee for your precious father."

I say nothing and head for the kitchen. As I'm making the coffee, she says, "I want all those dishes in the sink done, before your father gets home. When you're finished with that, you can peel potatoes for dinner." She's so demanding. She's so consumed with her own needs. Do this. Do that.

I feel like a slave. Will it never end?

I'm in the kitchen. I hear dad's voice. I'm so glad he's finally home. I yell out to him, "Hi, Dad."

He walks into the kitchen and asks, "How's my birth-day girl?"

I look at him and say, "My teacher, Mrs. Schaefer, had cupcakes for me, and everyone sang happy birthday. It was fun."

Dad looks at me and says, "I have something for my special little girl."

I say, "What is it?"

He says, "It's something that you asked for."

I say, " Where is it?"

Kathy says, "We will celebrate, after your father has had dinner."

She always has to stick her nose in everything. Why doesn't she just get lost?

Dinner is over, and the chores have been completed. I'm trying to be patient. I want so much to know what Dad got me.

Kathy walks into the kitchen and says, "Now we can have dessert."

I'm not sure what she is talking about; we never have dessert. I think to myself, "Maybe she made me a cake. But I doubt it."

She walks over to the stove, opens the oven door and reaches in.

I can't believe what I see. She pulls out a chocolate cake on a plate. I look at Junior, and he looks at me. I look at Kathy. I don't know what to say.

She breaks the silence and says, "Don't just stand there. Get some plates."

I move toward the cupboard.

Dad walks into the kitchen.

Kathy picks up the knife and is just about to cut the cake.

Dad says, "Wait, we have to have a candle for the birthday girl."

He places a candle in the middle of the cake and says, "Now, make a wish."

I look at Dad and say, "I don't know what to wish for."

He says, " You can wish for anything."

I close my eyes and wish Kathy would leave. I take a deep breath, open my eyes, blow out the candle, and hope my wish will be granted.

Dad says, "I have something very special for my little girl."

I look at him and ask, "What is it?"

He gets up from the table and walks into the living room, then returns with a long, wide box under his arm. He hands me the box and says, " Happy birthday."

The box is heavy. I wonder, "What could it be? "

Junior says, "Come on. Open it."

I put the box on the floor and pull the top off of it. To my surprise, it's a guitar.

I've always wanted one. I forgot I asked Dad for it a long time ago. He remembered. I look up at him and say, "Thank you." I sit, strumming the strings. It sure doesn't sound like music. It sounds funny. I guess, I'll need to learn how to tune and play it.

Kathy walks into the kitchen and says, "More noise in this house."

Can't she ever say something nice? All she does is complain, complain. I think to myself, "I'd rather hear music than the sound of the television."

I stand up, walk over to Dad and say, "I love you, Dad."

He puts his arms around and holds me tight.

It feels so good to be held. I don't want him to let go of me. Kathy walks back into the kitchen. Dad drops his arms and pulls away from me.

I think to myself, "Why does she always have to spoil things?"

Before going to bed, I walk over to the couch, where Dad is sitting. I look down at him, straight in the eyes and say, "I love you, Dad, and I really like the guitar."

He looks at me and says, "I love you, too."

Kathy is sitting on the other end of the couch and doesn't say a word.

I reach for him and give him a hug.

He kisses me on the forehead and says, "Goodnight."

With guitar in hand, I make my way to my room. Once there, I stand for a moment and contemplate. Where will I put it? Ah yes, over in the corner out of the way.

As I lay in my bed tonight, I hear Dad and Kathy talking in the other room.

I hear him tell her, "You shouldn't be so hard on her."

Kathy says, "Why? Because she is your precious little girl."

You're damn right. I'm his precious little girl! If only my birthday wish were to be granted. She would be gone, and we would be happy.

Chapter Nine
A Question Not Asked

June of 1966 would bring with it a three-day welcomed reprieve from Kathy. The birth of a child and time spent alone with Dad. A month later, at the age of twelve, I experience my first urinary tract infection.

On June 30, 1966, Kathy went into the hospital in the morning to have a baby. For the next three days, I'll be responsible for taking care of everyone. What a relief it is to have her out of the house. I'll have Dad all to myself. There will be no screaming or yelling. I won't have to jump to her every command. She is gone. At least for a couple of days, it will be quiet.

Dad comes to my room tonight. It's dark and quiet. Both Junior and Joey are in bed. He lies next to me without any clothes on. This is strange, because he usually wears his underwear. He turns on his side, facing me pulling me close.

I look at him and say, "I love you Dad."

He says, "I love you too," as he puts his hand between my legs rubbing me up and down. It feels good.

He takes my underwear off and puts his finger inside my vagina. It feels funny. He's never done this before. He moves his finger in and out. It hurts. I don't like it. I pull away. Dad's finger comes out. I rub my leg up against his penis.

This distracts him. It's hard and warm. He pulls my head down close to it. I already know what he wants me to do.

My mouth is around it. It smells awful. I try to pull my head up.

Dad has his hand on my head, pushing it down.

I get mad. Who does he think he is, pushing my head down? I bite it.

Dad says, "Ouch."

I pull my mouth off of it and say, "What?"

He says, "You have to be careful."

I say, "Oh, I'm sorry."

He doesn't realize I bit it intentionally. He has no idea how much I hate putting his smelly, ugly penis in my mouth. I put my mouth back on it at his request.

He lays there and says, "Squeeze it."

I squeeze it. I really want to squeeze it off! But, I know better.

He says, "Shake it."

I shake and squeeze at the same time. My arm starts to get sore. I ignore the pain. That awful tasting stuff comes out of his penis. I don't resist swallowing it. I know once the stuff comes out I won't have to do anything else.

The norm has been for him to get right up and leave my room. Tonight, he lays next to me for a very long time, holding me close. I feel the warmth of his body next to mine.

He doesn't say anything.

As I lay next to him, I wonder what he's thinking?

Although I like the attention I get from Dad while Kathy is gone, I am glad she is coming home from the hospital. After the third night of sleeping with him, I find myself looking forward to sleeping alone. My vagina is sore. I'm so glad he won't be sticking his fingers inside of me. It hurt so badly. I know, Dad loves and cares about me. But what I don't understand is why he never asks me, if it feels

81

good. I begin to wonder if he cares about what does and doesn't feel good to me. I'm not looking forward to hearing Kathy yell or scream at all. But I am excited to see the new baby, whom they named Michael.

A week has passed, since Kathy and Michael came home from the hospital. She's as mean as ever. It seems as if she has gotten moodier and meaner, since she had him. She screams and yells a lot more.

The second day they were home from the hospital, she taught me how to warm a bottle. Now when it is time for Michael to eat, she tells me to fix a bottle. I wonder how long it will be before I start feeding him.

Along with the birth of Michael come more demands and chores. She lets me know I am now responsible for making sure diapers do not sit in the diaper pail. I don't like this chore. The diapers smell, and they are so messy. She never rinses the diapers out, when Michael poops. I carry the diaper pail to the bathroom taking the cover off the pail. It smells so bad. I have to rinse the diapers out Michael pooped in. Placing my hand in the cold, dirty water in the toilet makes my stomach turn. I don't like to do this at all! Sometimes my hands smell of urine and poop for hours. It seems the smell just won't go away.

I haven't been feeling well for a couple of days. I tell Kathy my back hurts.

She says, "Stop being a baby. You just want attention from your dad."

I say nothing.

Another day passes. I go to Dad and tell him my back hurts.

He feels my forehead.

I have a fever. I tell him, "It hurts when I go pee."

Dad has concern in his voice and asks, "Why didn't you say something sooner?"

I whimper, "I told Kathy yesterday."

He says, "We have to go to the emergency room."

I say, "I don't want to go."

He tells me, "We're going."

Dad and I are in the car, driving to the hospital.

He tells me, "Someone at the hospital might ask you, if anyone has touched you."

I look at Dad and ask, "What do you mean?"

He says, "If anyone asks you about me touching you down there, you say no. Understand!"

I say, "Why would they ask?"

He says, "Remember our secret."

I say, "I will never tell."

Dad says, "If you tell them, you will be taken away."

I look at him and say, "I don't want them to take me away."

Dad says, "Don't say a word."

I say, "I won't."

I ask him, "Will you stay with me at the hospital?"

He says, "Yes, I won't leave your side."

I'm sitting on the gurney at the hospital, wearing this funny looking gown. It has an opening in the back. Dad and I are in this big room. There are other gurneys. The nurse comes in and asks me all kinds of questions.

The one question she fails to ask is, "Has anyone touched you?"

Before she leaves, she asks me to pee in a small cup for her.

I do as she asks.

She takes the cup and says, "I'll be back."

I sit on the gurney. I'm getting bored. It seems, like we have been at the hospital for hours. I look at Dad and say, "I want to leave."

He says, "We can't leave, until the Doctor sees you."

I ask, "Why does the Doctor need to see me?"

He says, "The Doctor needs to look at you, so he can give you medicine to help you feel better.

I ask, "What does the Doctor need to look at?"

Before Dad can answer me, I hear a deep voice say, "Hello."

A person in a white coat with a stethoscope around his neck appears.

He introduces himself to dad. The Doctor asks, "What's the problem?"

Dad says, "She's been running a fever, complaining it hurts when she urinates, and her lower back is very sore."

The Doctor walks over to the gurney and stands in front of me. He asks me to lay down.

I do as he asks.

He pushes on my lower stomach and asks, "Does this hurt?"

I say, "No."

He listens to my heart, then my lungs and asks me to sit up. I'm relieved. I am so glad he didn't look at my privates.

He asks me, "Take some deep breaths."

I suck in the air and blow it out.

He says, "Your heart and lungs sound good and are clear." The Doctor looks at dad and says, "I need to see, if the results of the urinalysis came back. I'll be back soon." The Doctor returns a few minutes later. He doesn't talk to me, but directly to dad. "She has a urinary tract infection and it is uncommon for someone of her age. I am prescribing some medication that should help her feel better within twenty-four hours."

I say, "Can we leave now?"

The Doctor looks at me and says; "Yes, you can leave."

The Doctor walks out of the room; I jump off the gurney, take off the funny looking gown and rush to put my clothes on.

As we are walking to the car, Dad tells me we have to stop at the drug store to get the prescription filled, before we go home.

As we drive to the drug store, dad says, "You must never tell anyone what we do."

I look at him and say, "I won't. I promise!"

He smiles at me and says, "You are my special little girl."

I look at him and say nothing.

When we arrive home and walk through the door, Kathy demands to know, "Where were you two for so long?"

Dad says, "We were at the hospital. Where did you think we were?"

Kathy with suspicion in her voice says, "It shouldn't have taken you that long."

Dad says nothing.

Kathy starts yelling at him. The yells become louder. I bet the neighbors can hear her.

I walk through the living room to the bathroom.

Dad is sitting on the couch, smoking a cigarette.

After using the toilet, I stand at the bathroom door. I'm afraid to open it. If she sees me, she will start screaming for sure.

I talk myself into opening the door. I take a deep breath, grab the handle, and pull the door towards me. I don't look at Dad, but look straight ahead. I make it to my room without her saying a word to me. I don't know how he can just sit there and listen to her yell.

Her voice gets louder and louder. "You and your precious little girl. What, do you have a thing for her?"

I get nervous and wonder, if she knows what Dad and I do? I listen.

I hear Dad say, "Shut up!"

Kathy yells louder and says, "You spoil her. You let her get away with everything. You love her more than me."

I hear Dad yell back at her and say, "Shut up or I will leave."

It becomes quiet. The yelling has finally stopped.

This would be the first of many trips to the emergency room due to a urinary tract infection. Although I clearly understood the importance of keeping our SECRET, I secretly wished someone would ask, "Did your Dad touch you?" No one ever asked. The secret remained a secret.

Chapter Ten

Rage

Over the next few years, Kathy's true self would emerge. Her verbal abuse quickly turns into physical abuse. Bringing with it a visit from a social worker and yet another move.

On Labor Day weekend 1967, I'm excited. School will be starting in just a few days. I can't wait to get away from the house. Instead of the summer being fun and restful, it's been long and upsetting. Going to school will be a welcomed break.

I am not only Kathy's personal slave all day long, but I also have the responsibility of taking care of Michael. I feel like he's my baby, instead of hers. Once he turns six months old, I become his primary caretaker. He begins to turn to me for his every need. I think, this happens, because he too becomes afraid of her. When I look into his dark brown eyes, I can see the fear. When I hold him in my arms after or during one of Kathy's yelling or screaming rampages, I can feel his body shake. Though my responsibilities increase, I am thankful. I learned that as long as Michael was in my arms, there would be a slim chance of Kathy hitting me. The lesson is learned in error.

One day when Michael is fourteen months old, because I don't move fast enough, she grabs my hair, pulls it and says, " The next time you will move faster!"

God, it feels as if though she is pulling my hair right out of my head. It hurt so badly. I now know, if I hear

Michael cry, to go running. He and I have become one another's safe haven.

Junior is just as happy as I am to return to school.

It seems like Kathy is screaming and yelling at him all the time. When she yells at him, he yells back. She doesn't like this. She has begun to get into physical fights with him. If he sasses back, she hits him. A number of times when he's on the other side of the room, she picks something up and throws it at him. She slaps him in the face, kicks him and sometimes doubles up her fist and punches him.

I watch and know not to say a word. I don't want her hitting me like that.

Joey usually stands off to one side of the room. He watches. He doesn't say a word. He looks scared.

I've been back in school for a couple of weeks. It feels good. When I'm there, I don't think about anyone at home. There's no yelling, screaming or having to take care of Michael.

My teacher's name is Mrs. Hubby. She's an older lady with gray hair and glasses. She's nice and I like her. When she speaks, she speaks softly. She doesn't raise her voice.

I never look forward to having to go home in the afternoon. I wish school were all day and all night. I have no friends.

Right after school I have to go home. Kathy gives me fifteen minutes to get there. If I'm not home on time, I get into trouble. Today, I arrive home one minute late. As I walk in the door, Kathy starts screaming at me. She demands to know where I was and what I was doing.

I look at her and say, "I was walking home from school."

She says, "No you weren't. You're late!"

I say, "Yes I was."

She says, "Don't talk back at me." She grabs my hair and pulls it.

I try to get away.

She yanks me towards her and slaps me in the face.

I begin to cry.

She lets go of my hair.

My head hurts. I can't stop crying.

She tells me, "Go to your room, and change your clothes."

I run to my room and close the door. I can't stop crying. She is such a mean bitch! I throw myself on the bed. I hear her yell, "You better hurry up, or you'll get it again!"

Throughout the summer of 1968, Kathy would become more and more violent. Pulling of the hair and slaps in the face ended. She now uses her fist and objects to control. She instills the fear of God in all of us. She doesn't seem to hit me as often. I think, its because I am caring for both Michael and Joey.

Junior, on the other hand, tends to be the recipient of most of her rage.

Dad is of no help. He works during the week and now has a part-time job on Friday and Saturday evenings. It seems he is oblivious to any and all things that happen at home.

In mid-August it finally happens! Kathy has really hurt Junior. The incident occurs right after lunch.

Junior and I are clearing off the table.

Kathy says to Junior, "Move faster."

He says, "I'm going fast enough."

Kathy yells, "Don't talk back at me."

He says, "Why? Are you going to hit me?" He's standing at the table.

She is sitting in the chair. Kathy stands up, grabs the glass bowl the tuna fish was in, and hits him over the head with it.

I can't believe what she has just done.

Glass goes flying everywhere. Junior is crying.

I see blood dripping down the side of his face.

I start to cry. I can feel my body begin to shake.

Kathy yells, "Get a towel!"

I run into the bathroom, grab a towel and run back out into the other room.

She grabs it from my hand and tells Junior, "Get over here."

She puts the towel on the top of his head and tells me, "Get some ice out of the freezer."

My body feels numb from the fear I feel. I move as quickly as I can. She yanks the ice from me and places it on Junior's head. There's blood all over the place.

God, I hope he's going to be okay.

She tells me, "Hand me the phone." She calls dad at work and tells him there has been an accident and he needs to come home right now. The time that lapses between the phone call and dad's arrival home seems short.

He walks in the door and asks, "What happened?"

Kathy begins to speak, but Junior cuts her off and says, "She broke the bowl over my head for no reason."

Kathy says, "It was an accident."

Dad looks at Junior and says, "Come on. I need to get you to the Doctor."

As dad walks by me, I ask, "Can I go?"

He says, "No, you need to stay here."

It seems like dad and Junior have been gone for hours. I wish they would get home. I'm worried. I wonder if Junior is okay, if he had to have stitches.

Kathy hasn't said a word to me the entire time they have been gone. She sits on the couch and watches that stupid television. She seems, like she is in her own little world.

That's okay; at least she won't bug me. As I stand at the sink doing the lunch dishes, I hear voices. It sounds like dad, so I peak around the corner. Dad is standing next to the couch.

Junior sees me and walks towards the kitchen. He has a bandage wrapped around his head. He walks into the room and says, "I got four stitches because of that bitch."

I whisper, "Hush! She will hear you."

He says, "I don't care. I hate her."

I look at him and say, "Me too. I can't wait for school to start."

Dinner is pretty quiet this evening, actually enjoyable. Kathy wasn't sarcastic or demanding, as she so often is at mealtime. Instead, she doesn't say a word. She probably feels bad. She should, after what she did!

I wonder how long the calmness will last.

Ah, its September. The first day of school has finally arrived. Excitement and thankfulness fill my total being. I'm careful not to make any noise this morning, while getting ready for school. I don't want her to get up and ruin my day, before it has begun. I don't walk to school and talk about the new clothes I have gotten or the nervousness I feel about the first day of school. Instead, both Junior and I talk about Kathy.

As we are walking to school, I ask, "Why is she so mean?"

He says, "She was born mean."

I say, "I'm afraid of her. One day she is going to hurt me."

91

He says, "One day I will beat her up."

I say, "She is so big."

He laughs and says, "She is a fat cow."

I chuckle and say, "A cow is much nicer."

He turns, looks at me and says, "One day, I will get her." He has such a serious determined look on his face.

If that day ever comes, I'll be right there, cheering him on. She would finally get what she deserves.

Once again, school has become my great escape. There I'm not nervous, and my stomach doesn't tighten up. I don't worry about someone yelling at me. I don't wonder when she will scream at me. No one slaps me in the face, pulls my hair or beats me.

As the school day passes and morning turns into afternoon, I begin to think about going home. My stomach gets tight. I feel nauseous.

We've been in school for about one month. It is October of 1968. We arrive home. As we walk in the door, Kathy looks at Junior and says, "Because of you welfare is here. She is going to take you away."

There is this lady sitting at the kitchen table. I've not seen her before. She has long dark hair. She's pretty. As I look into her eyes, I notice they're soft and have a twinkle to them. I wonder who she is.

Junior looks at Kathy and says, "No one is going to take me away!"

Both Junior and I walk into the other room.

I listen to hear what is being said. I hear Kathy tell this person we will be moving. I hear her say the neighbors are liars and troublemakers.

I wasn't aware we were going to move.

I hear Kathy say, "He deserves what he gets!"

I wonder if she is here because of the black eyes and marks Kathy has left on Junior.

Kathy's voice becomes very loud. I hear her tell this person to leave.

God, I hope she doesn't leave, until Dad gets home.

I hear the lady say, "If you want me to leave, I will."

No, she can't leave. There's no telling what Kathy will do.

I hear the door slam.

Kathy walks into the living room. She looks at Junior and says, "You bastard! You got me into trouble. I hope they take you away." She looks at both of us and says, "Go to your rooms."

Without any hesitation, I make my way there. Please, I hope, dad comes home soon! I bet, one of the neighbors finally called someone. They are probably just as tired as I am of hearing her scream and yell. I hear footsteps. Maybe Dad is home. I stand at my door and listen to the voices. I hear his voice. I open my door. They're in the living room. Kathy starts yelling.

I hear her say, "Welfare was here today. I told her she could take him away."

I hear Dad ask, "Why was she here, and what was her name?"

Kathy screams at him and says, "Her name was Diane Meier. She was here, because I beat him. Someone saw the marks. The next time I will kill him."

Ah, I was right. Someone did call. I wonder who saw the marks.

I hear Dad say in a very loud voice, "You will keep your hands off of him! I told you someday someone would see the marks."

93

Tonight, as I lay in my bed, I pray Dad will come to see me. I think about the lady, who came to the house today. I wonder if she'll be back. I wonder if she'll talk to me. I wonder if she will make Kathy stop being so mean to us. Probably not, everyone is afraid of her.

I hear my door open. It's Dad. I stand up. I reach for him. He wraps his arms around me. I hold onto him and cry.

He asks, "What's wrong?"

I say, "I am afraid of Kathy. She is mean to us all the time. If that lady comes to the house again and asks me what Kathy does to us, I am going to tell her."

He says, "You don't say anything to anyone!"

I say, "But she is so mean."

Dad pulls away from me. "You don't say anything to anyone. If you say anything, they will take you away."

I look at him and say, "I won't. Is it true we are moving?"

He asks, "Who told you that?"

I say, "I heard Kathy tell that lady we were moving."

He says, "Yes."

I ask, "Why?"

He says, "Because the neighbors are so nosey." He draws me close and wraps his arms around me. We stand in silence for a few minutes. He says, "Kathy will be getting out of the tub. I have to go."

I say, "I love you, Dad."

He says, "I love you too."

He turns and walks out of the room.

I climb back into bed. This is the first night ever he's not made me do something. I didn't have to put it in my mouth. I didn't have to shake it. He didn't put his fingers inside of me. I roll over on my stomach. I wrap my arms around my pillow and say, "Thank you, God."

Chapter Eleven
Please, Take Me Too

The following months would bring with it frequent visits from the welfare department. In April 1969, my sounding board and best friend would be taken away.

It's the weekend, and we have moved into the new apartment. The day has been long and busy. The apartment has its plus and minuses. A plus is that we live in the basement apartment, no more climbing three flights of stairs. I have my own bedroom that is off the living room. Junior has his own room that is off the kitchen. Joey and Michael share a room that is off Dad and Kathy's room, which is right off the living room.

Dad was very creative and put up a divider to separate their room from the living room, I guess, so they could have some privacy. The only thing I don't like about the apartment is that all the windows that face the apartment building to the left of our apartment have bars on them. When I look out my bedroom window, I see bars. I've not seen bars on apartment windows before and wonder why they are there.

I ask Dad why?

He tells me the landlord put them on the windows, so the troublemakers in the apartment building next door wouldn't bother us.

I wonder to myself, "Are we going to be safe?"

Although, the street is busy and many people are coming and going as we unload the boxes, no one takes the time to stop and say hi. They look and just go on their merry way.

Dad, Junior and I spend most of our day, moving our belongings from the truck into the apartment. As we carry boxes into the apartment, Kathy unpacks them and puts things away.

I feel bad for Michael and Joey. It seems, like most of the day Kathy is yelling at them to get out of her way.

I am surprised she didn't make me watch the boys. Then I think to myself, "If I watched the boys, she would have to carry boxes from the truck to the apartment. She is too lazy to do that."

The apartment is all situated. Everything is put away. The beds are set up.

I am glad the day has finally come to an end. My body is tired and sore from lifting all those boxes.

Ah, it feels good to finally, be in my bed. The smells and sounds are all new. I can hear loud voices coming from the apartment building next door. It sounds, like two people yelling at one another. I wonder if I will hear this all the time. The smell of fresh paint fills the air of my room and the apartment. Even though I am tired, it takes me a long time to fall asleep.

I hear Dad and Kathy's voices coming from the living room. I can't hear what they are saying. The television is too loud. I think about getting up and putting my ear to the door. I decide not to. If Kathy should hear me, I know I will get into trouble.

The yelling from next door has stopped. Either Dad or Kathy turned off the television. It is quiet.

I think maybe now I can fall asleep. I turn over on my stomach, hug my pillow and say good night to God.

Junior and I no longer attend the same school. He goes to an elementary school and is in the sixth grade. I attend a middle school and am in the seventh grade. I am not happy about this. It was pleasant walking to and from school with him. I always looked forward to this time we had with one another. A lot of the time, we would talk about Kathy. It was our time to be able to vent to one another. We would tell each other how we felt. Dad wouldn't listen to our complaints, so we complained to one another. After we complained, we would call her all kinds of names and make fun of her. We would take turns pretending we were telling her off. We would laugh.

I would always feel better. I really miss not having that time with him.

I've been at the new school now for about a month and a half. School lets out at 2:50 p.m. I have to be home no later than 3:15p.m. I haven't made any friends. This is okay. I don't really have any time for friends. I rush home. I know not to be late. I don't want Kathy to scream or yell at me. I don't want her to hit me. I hope she is in a good mood.

Today, as I walk down our street and get closer to home, I speed up my walk and know that everything will be okay. Dad is home. I'm standing in front of the house. I hear Kathy screaming. I wonder, "What is wrong?"

I take a deep breath and walk down the three concrete stairs, then the short distance to the door. Grabbing the handle, I turn it and push the door open. As I walk in, dad and Kathy are in the living room. When they both look in my direction, I wonder, "Am I in trouble?"

Kathy raises her voice and says, "Your precious little girl is home. I hope they take her away too."

I stand in the kitchen, not knowing what to say or do.

Dad looks at Kathy and says, "It's because of you they have taken Junior away."

Kathy says, "Look at her. She so is pathetic."

I say nothing, but stand in silence.

Dad looks at Kathy and asks, "Are you coming with me?"

Kathy speaks very loudly and says, "She came to the house this morning and gave me those papers. Who the hell does she think she is? Yes, I want to go see her. I'm going to give Diane Meier what she deserves."

I stand in the kitchen and think to myself, "Is this the lady that came to the house before?" She must have come back. I wonder what happened.

Dad looks at me and says, "Take care of Michael and Joey. We will be back"

I look at Dad and ask, "Where is Junior? "

He says, "They took him from school."

I ask, "Who took him?"

He says, "The Welfare people."

I ask, "Is he coming home?"

He says, "I don't know."

Kathy walks into the kitchen, looks at Dad and says, "Let's go." Kathy looks at me and says, "Nothing better happen to them." She opens the door and walks out.

Dad doesn't say anything. He doesn't look at me, but follows a short distance behind her out the door.

Dad and Kathy return to the house a couple hours later. Junior isn't with them.

I ask Dad if Junior is coming home?

He looks at me and says, "No."

Kathy doesn't say anything. I wonder what happened. I wonder if Kathy got into trouble.

I ask Dad, "When will Junior come home?"

He looks at me with tears in his eyes. "We have to go to court, then he will come home."

I look at Dad and tell him, "I want Junior to come home. Do you know where he is? "

Dad says, "He is in a foster home."

I ask, "What is a foster home? "

Dad tells me, "It's a home."

I wonder what kind of home it is. I wonder if the people are going to be nice to him. I wonder if they are as mean as Kathy. I wonder if I will ever see him again. Dad said he would come home after the court date. I hope it's soon. I miss him.

Kathy is pretty quiet the entire evening. She sits in front of the television, smoking cigarette after cigarette. I do the chores. We have dinner.

I give both Michael and Joey baths, then put them to bed. Michael doesn't want me to leave the room. He lies on his stomach. I rub his back. He falls asleep. I tiptoe out of their room. As I walk through Dad and Kathy's bedroom and into the living room, Kathy doesn't say a word to me. She doesn't even look at me, but stares at the television.

I think to myself, "Maybe she is scared?"

I hear the tub water running in the bathroom. I lay in bed, wondering if Dad is going to come to my room.

My bedroom door opens. It's Dad. He has a paper towel in his hand.

I know what this means. He stands next to my bed. He pulls his penis out of his pants.

I sit up. His penis goes in my mouth. Although the skin that covers his penis is soft and warm, his penis is hard.

Dad says, " Shake it."

I shake it. I don't want it in my mouth. I don't want to shake it. I want to talk to Dad about Kathy. I want to tell him all about what she does and says to us.

The awful stuff comes out. He has one of his hands on the back of my head. He is pushing me forward.

I am forced to swallow that awful stuff.

Dad pulls his penis out of my mouth putting it in his pants. He says, "I have to go. She's out of the tub."

When he closes my door, I lay there. I am not very happy. I begin to think he cares more about Kathy than Junior or I.

The next day shortly after I arrive home from school, Diane Meier comes to the house.

I am preparing a pot of coffee for Dad in the electric percolator. Dad should be home shortly.

Kathy tells her she can sit at the table. So she does.

I look at her while I am fixing the coffee.

She sits at the table quietly, not looking at me.

I wonder if she will talk to me. I hope so. Then, I can tell her about how mean Kathy is. I can tell her Junior should come home and she should take Kathy away.

Michael distracts me by hanging on my leg. I look down at him. He looks up at me and asks for some strawberry milk.

I make my way to the cupboard to get his favorite glass. As he starts to cry, I tell him I am coming. I put the strawberry powdered stuff in the glass, then get the milk out of the refrigerator. I pour the milk into the glass.

While Michael is hanging onto my leg, I grab a spoon from the dish drainer and stir what is in the glass, before putting it on the table. I pull the chair out, lift Michael up and put him on the chair. Michael doesn't waste anytime.

He reaches for the glass, draws it to his mouth and begins to drink it.

The kitchen door opens. Dad has just arrived home.

Kathy looks at me and says, "Take the kids in the other room. This is grown up talk."

I do as she asks. As I am walking out of the kitchen, I look at Dad.

He says nothing.

I look at Diane Meier. She looks at me. I feel the warmth that generates from her soft, sensitive eyes. She looks strong, but I can tell she is afraid of Kathy. Although her eyes are soft and sensitive, I recognize the look of fear I know all too well. She doesn't say a word.

I take Michael and Joey into the living room and turn on the television. Both boys sit down and are distracted.

As I'm sitting on the couch, I try to hear what is being said in the kitchen.

Kathy says, "Junior is a troublemaker. He has a big mouth."

She is a big liar. I wish someone would ask me what happens around here.

I hear Diane Meier tell Dad and Kathy there is a court date. She lets them know she and Junior will be there.

I wonder when they are going to court. I listen. I can't hear all they are saying. I only hear bits and pieces.

Michael and Joey are laughing at the cartoons on the television. It is too noisy to hear everything that is being said in the other room.

I hear her say good bye to Dad and Kathy. Finally, the door opens, then closes. She has gone without saying good bye to me or the boys. I wonder if she will be back.

Junior has been gone for almost a week. I miss him and wish he were home.

I hear dad tell Kathy they will be going to court in the morning. I wonder if this means Junior will be coming home. I hope so.

Dad gets me up in the morning for school. I am standing in the kitchen. Kathy is still in bed.

I whisper, "Is Junior coming home?"

He says, "I hope so."

I say, "Me too."

He says, "I have to go." He walks towards the door, opens it and closes it quietly.

I stand in the kitchen and think about Junior. I miss, not combing his hair in the morning. I miss, telling him that he is handsome. I miss, being able to talk to him. I am careful not to make any noise. I don't want Kathy to wake up. After I finish getting myself ready for school, I make myself a sandwich for lunch and miss not making a sandwich for Junior. I grab my jacket, books and lunch, open the door carefully and think to myself, "Please don't let her wake up."

It is a chilly morning. The street is quiet. I hear the sound of chirping birds, as I walk to school. I wish I could be a bird and fly away. There would be no more beatings. Kathy couldn't call me a pathetic pimple faced bitch. There wouldn't be any more screaming or yelling. I wouldn't be treated like a slave. I wouldn't have to put dad's penis in my mouth and taste that awful stuff.

Dad wouldn't be able to hurt me any more with his fingers. There wouldn't be any more secrets.

I think about Michael and Joey. Even if it were possible for me to fly away, I wouldn't. I need to stay and take care of them. As I get closer to school, I have a conversation with God. I ask him to please let Junior come home. I tell him how much I miss my brother.

As I walk home from school today, I think about Junior. Dad said that they were going to court today.

I wonder if Junior is home. I speed up my walk down our street. I look to see if Dad's car is parked in front of the house. I don't see it. I wish he were home. I stand in front of the house, wondering if Kathy is in a good mood and if Junior is home. I take a deep breath, open the door to the apartment and walk in.

Michael and Joey come running to me. Michael holds onto my legs, looks up at me and says, "Up."

I bend down to pick him up, wrapping my arms around him and lifting him to my chest. Joey looks up at me.

I say, " Hi."

He smiles.

Kathy is in the living room.

I don't see Junior. I wonder what happened in court.

Kathy tells me, "Give the boys a snack."

I have both Michael and Joey sit at the kitchen table. I give them some milk and cookies, as I think to myself, "She is so fat and lazy." I rinse out the coffeepot, fill it with water, place the coffee in it, then plug it in. The coffee will be ready for dad, when he gets home.

I hear voices outside. The door opens. Dad walks in. Junior is right behind him.

I am standing near the kitchen sink. I walk around the table towards Junior feeling tears rolling down my face. I reach for Junior. He reaches for me. We hold onto one another for what seems to be a long time. I am crying and at the same time telling him how much I've missed him.

Junior tells me he missed me too.

Kathy walks into the kitchen.

Junior and I let go of one another.

She stands for a minute, not saying a word. She looks at Junior and I.

Dad is fixing himself a cup of coffee.

The boys are sitting at the table, finishing up their snack.

She says in a very loud mean tone, "The next time I will have you both taken away."

Junior and I look at one another and say nothing.

Dad looks at Kathy and says, "Shut your mouth!"

She walks into the other room.

I can tell that she is mad.

Dad doesn't say anything else.

I'm glad. What dad doesn't know is that when he and she argue and he goes off to work, she takes all her anger out on us. She is such a coward.

Dad quit his part-time job, so he could be home more. He is only working his full-time job.

I'm glad. I'm not as afraid of Kathy, when he is home. Things don't get better at the house. I thought that maybe they would, because dad is home more. Kathy makes me do everything around the house. I feel like "Cinderella." If I'm not cleaning, getting dinner ready, doing wash, I'm taking care of both Michael and Joey. The only break I get is school and sleep.

I have a friend that I met at school. Margaret lives up the street from us. She is so nice. We walk to school together every day. She waits for me at the corner in the morning. Sometimes we get to walk home together. This doesn't happen very often. Margaret is very involved in school activities. When we do walk home together, we talk and laugh.

She asks me one day, "Can you come to my house after school?"

I tell her, "I can't."

She asks, "Why? "

I tell her, "I have to get home to do chores and take care of my brothers."

She says, "I will come to your house to help you with your chores."

I say, "No," and think to myself, "I don't want her to meet Kathy."

One day as Margaret and I are walking to school, she says, "I was walking past your house the other day and heard lots of screaming."

I say, "It was probably Kathy."

Margaret asks, "Does she scream all the time?"

I say, "Yes."

She asks, "How can you stand it? "

I look at her and say, "I can't. I don't like Kathy. She is mean all the time."

She says, "People on the street talk about her."

I ask, "What do they say? "

She says, "They say she doesn't let you do anything. They say they always hear screaming, cries and her yelling all the time."

I don't say anything and continue to walk.

Margaret asks, "Is this true? "

I say, "Yes."

We turn the corner onto our street. Margaret lives in the corner house. I live further down. We look at one another.

She says, "I'll see you in the morning."

I say, "Bye."

As I walk the short distance from Margaret's house to mine, I wonder if Kathy will be in a good mood. Once I get home, I rush to change my clothes and complete my chores.

Kathy seems to be in a good mood. Instead of standing in the kitchen waiting for me to arrive, she was sitting on the couch in front of the television, watching one of her talk shows. This is always a good sign.

As I finish making the coffee, I decide I will ask her, if Margaret can come to the house. I walk into the living room, look at her and ask, "Can my friend Margaret come to the house?"

Without turning her head to look at me, she asks, "Where does she live?"

I say, "Up the street."

Kathy asks, "How do you know her? "

I say, "I walk to school with her everyday."

She says, "What do you mean you walk to school with her."

I can feel my stomach muscles begin to tighten up. Oh no, I'm in trouble. She doesn't know I don't walk to school alone. I look at her and say, "I walk to school with her every day."

To my surprise she doesn't yell or scream at me. Instead, without taking her eyes off the television screen she says, "Yes."

I ask, "When?"

She says, "Tomorrow."

I am so excited. I can't wait to see Margaret in the morning to tell her the good news.

The next morning Margaret is waiting for me at the corner, as she usually does.

I look at her and say, "Kathy said you could come to the house today after school."

Margaret says, "Really."

I say, "Yeah."

We get to school. I say good bye to Margaret. She says good bye to me. I walk to my classroom. I am so excited. Margaret is the first friend I have had, since we moved from the country to the city.

Throughout the school day my thoughts drift. God, I hope Kathy is nice to Margaret and doesn't yell or scream, while my friend is at the house. Ah, it should be okay. Dad will be home at four.

As Margaret and I walk home from school together, she lets me know she will bring her guitar.

I let her know I am not very good at playing mine.

She lets me know it doesn't matter.

We arrive on our street.

Margaret tells me she has to change her clothes and tell her mother where she is going to be. She tells me she would be down in a little while.

I look at her and say, "Okay. I will see you then."

I walk down the street with my head up. My stomach muscles aren't tightening up. My body doesn't feel heavy. I'm not dreading getting home.

I walk in the door.

Both Michael and Joey come running to me.

I bend down, hug them and say, " Hi."

Kathy sits on the couch, watching a talk show.

I rush to my room to change my clothes. I need to hurry, because I want to get all my chores done, before Margaret arrives. As I am making my way to the kitchen, I walk past her.

Just before I reach the kitchen she says, "You better start peeling those potatoes."

I feel my stomach muscles begin to tighten. Oh no, don't tell me she has forgotten Margaret is coming.

I turn, look at her and say, "My friend Margaret is coming to the house."

She says, "Don't talk back to me."

I don't say a word, but walk into the kitchen. I know I must hurry. Margaret will be here soon. I get a pot from the cupboard to put the potatoes in. Then I remember I have to get the coffee ready for Dad. I think I will be able to get everything done, before Margaret gets here.

The coffee is made. The potatoes are peeled. I hear a knock on the door.

Kathy says, "Who is at the damn door? "

I say, "I think, it's my friend Margaret."

She says, "See who it is. "

I go to the door and open it. It's Margaret. She looks scared.

I wonder how long she has been standing there. I wonder if she heard everything that Kathy said. I hope not.

I look at her and say, "Come in." Oh no, she has her guitar. It's been so long, since I've played mine. I hope I can just listen and not play.

She looks at me and says, "I thought we could play our guitars."

I look at her and say, "I don't play well."

She says, "I can teach you."

My hard callous fingertips no longer exist. Instead, they are soft and sensitive. It's been months, since I last picked up my guitar. I look at her and say, "Okay, let me go get my guitar."

I walk out of the kitchen, through the living room, and into my bedroom. My guitar is sitting in the corner of my room. I reach for it. I notice it is dusty. I wipe it off with my hand. God, it's been so long, since I last picked it up. I walk out of my room with guitar in hand.

Margaret is sitting in a chair at the kitchen table.

Michael and Joey are standing next to her.

I pull a chair out from the table and put my guitar on my knee.

Michael wants to get on my lap.

I tell him he can't sit on my lap.

He starts to cry.

I put the guitar down and pick him up putting him on my lap. I know better than to let him cry. I don't want Kathy to start screaming.

Margaret strums the strings on her guitar. She sings the song "The House of the Rising Sun." She has such a pretty voice. " Come on. Now you try."

I put Michael down.

He starts to cry.

I pick him back up. I ask both boys, "Do you want some cookies and milk?"

They both nod.

I get them situated at the table. We should be all set. I reach for my guitar.

Kathy walks into the kitchen, looks at me and says, "Your friend has to leave. We are going to have dinner."

I look at Margaret.

She looks at me.

I don't know what to say. Dad isn't even home. What does she mean we're going to have dinner. We never have dinner, before he gets home.

Margaret stands up. She has her guitar in her hand. "I'll see you in morning."

I say, "Okay."

She turns to her right, grabs the door handle and pulls it towards her. As it opens, Margaret walks out.

Kathy doesn't say a word.

I wish she had watched Michael and Joey, while Margaret was here. She only came to the house a few more times. Quite often when she came to the house, Kathy would be yelling at Junior or saying mean things to him. Other times, I would have to take care of both Michael and Joey, while we were visiting. Usually, Margaret looked as scared as I felt, when Kathy raised her voice. She told me one day as we were walking to school that she wouldn't be coming to the house anymore.

I asked her, "Why?"

She told me, "I'm afraid of her. She yells and is so mean."

I remember looking at Margaret, holding back my tears and saying, " Me too."

Margaret and I continued to walk to school daily. She remained my friend in spite of her fear of Kathy.

Things don't get better at the home. Junior is always getting into trouble at school.

Kathy is complaining, yelling or hitting one of us. Most times, the only reprieve I have is in the evening, when Dad is home.

But, lately that hasn't even happened. It seems like he and Kathy are arguing all the time. I feel like I am losing my mind.

The person from welfare, Diane Meier, comes to the house quite often.

I wish so badly that she would talk to me.

She just looks at me and smiles.

Can't she see I'm not happy? I want her to ask me how I feel about things. I want her to ask me what really goes on in this house.

But she doesn't. Instead, she sits at the kitchen table and talks to Kathy. The crisis in our family seems to have drawn them both together. It appears that Kathy has a friend, but things haven't gotten better at home.

Today, I hear them talking about an institution for Junior. I think to myself, "Kathy is the one who needs an institution." I wonder why this lady doesn't talk to me. Why doesn't she ask me how I am. Why does she spend all her time with Kathy? Could there be some truth to what Kathy says? Am I really just a pathetic pimple faced bitch?

In April of 1969, I am very sad. Dad and Kathy yell and argue with one another all the time.

I hear Kathy tell dad, "If you don't put him away, then I am leaving. " Kathy blames everything on Junior.

Dad has agreed to send Junior to an institution.

I can't believe he is doing this.

It seems like both dad and this person from the Welfare Department never really pay attention to what is really going on. Junior is the one, who always has the bruises.

I tell dad what Kathy does to us, and he does nothing. Dad has always told me no one would ever take us away. Junior is going away. Dad has lied to me. I wonder if I will be next.

The day has arrived that Junior leaves. Diane Meier comes to the house to pick him up.

I stare at her.

She stands tall, speaks slowly and softly, and lets Junior know they need to leave. Finally, she glances at me, then looks away. She assures Dad and Kathy Junior is going to be fine.

Dad looks sad with tears in his eyes.

Kathy looks relieved.

Michael and Joey know Junior is leaving. They don't seem to be upset. I don't think they understand why he is going away or realize how long he will be gone.

As Junior and Diane Meier walk out the door, I feel as if though I have lost my best friend. I can feel the warm tears rolling down my cheeks. Who will I be able to talk to about Kathy? I wonder if the people at the institution will beat him, like Kathy does. I wonder if Kathy will hit me more. I wish we were both going away.

Chapter Twelve
A Memorable Evening

The spring and summer of 1970 would bring with it much turmoil. I meet someone, who found me to be attractive, but know the relationship will never develop. The overwhelming competition between Kathy and I would bring the loss of my virginity. I would enter womanhood without having a choice.

In the spring of 1970, it seems like all I do is wake up, go to school, come home and take care of everyone. I feel, like Cinderella without her Prince in shining armor.

Kathy hasn't changed a bit. She is so demanding, always finding something about which to complain.

I've never heard her say thank you or compliment anyone. These things are unheard of in this household. She still yells and screams.

I'm sure that the neighbors must hear her. I wonder, what they say about her. I wonder, what they think of her. I wonder, why no one says something to her.

She is so loud and so self-centered. Lately when she gets mad at me even for the tiniest things, she pulls my hair and smacks my face. If I say anything to her or look at her the wrong way, the smacks turn into punches. I have learned to keep my mouth shut. I know better.

A few years ago, she would only call me a "pathetic pimple faced bitch," when she got really mad at me. Now she says it to me all the time.

I don't like it, when I hear those words come out of her mouth. I cry, feel bad and look into the mirror, seeing all

113

the pimples on my face. I don't look pretty. I don't feel pretty.

Quite often Dad or Kathy will send me to the corner store to get milk or a loaf of bread. I like this. It gets me out of the apartment for a little while.

Sometimes neighborhood boys are hanging out on the corner. When I walk by, one of them will usually say, "Hi."

I smile and don't say anything. I've been instructed not to speak to anyone.

Either Kathy or Dad usually stand in front of the house and watch me walk to and from the store. I wonder, what they think I am going to do.

I like it, when Pedro who lives next door to us is hanging out with them. He always says, "Hi."

I don't utter a word or look at him. I can feel the blood rush to my head and my face grows warm. I think to myself, "Someone said hi. I must not be that ugly."

Margaret and I still walk to school in the morning. Although I never talk to her about what happens at home, she becomes a source of comfort and stability for me. She never raises her voice. She doesn't say mean things to me or ask anything of me. She is simply my friend, the only friend I have.

One day, she introduces me to her brother Mark, who is cute, quiet and nice. He goes to the same school we do. A short time after the initial introduction, he begins to walk to and from school with me on a daily basis.

I like this.

Margaret begins to become very active in school sports and goes to the girls' club quite often after school. One day she asks me to come with her.

I let her know that I can't. I must get home right after school. I have to take care of the boys.

Mark isn't as active in after school activities, so we continue our walks home together. I don't tell Dad or Kathy he and I walk to and from school together. It's none of their business. He is my friend. As long as I get home right after school, they will never know.

Mark and I talk about how hard it is to do algebra. It seems neither one of us have been able to master it. He tells lots of funny jokes. I laugh at most of them. He doesn't yell or get angry. He is such a happy go lucky person.

The school year is coming to an end. I am sad. This means that I won't see Margaret or Mark, until school begins in the fall. The last day of school, as Mark and I are walking home, I let him know I will see him, as soon as school begins in the fall.

He turns to me and says, "You only live down the street. We can see one another during the summer."

I say, "No. I have to watch my brothers."

He says, "Don't you get to do anything?"

I say, "No."

He says, "Maybe, we can go to dinner."

Go to dinner? No one has ever asked me to go out to dinner before. I've never been on a date.

With nervousness in my voice I say, "If Kathy or Dad found out we walked to and from school together, I would get into trouble."

He says, "Everyone talks about how mean Kathy is. Are you afraid of her?"

I look at him and say, "Yes."

Mark says, "I will miss you."

I say, "I will miss you too. Summer will pass quickly."

As he and I are standing in front of his house, I look at him and say, "I have to go. I can't be late."

Mark looks at me and says, "Take care."

I walk away. As I hurry down the street, I think about him. It sure would be nice to go to dinner with him. I've never been out with anyone. I will miss our conversations about algebra, but don't think either one of us will miss algebra itself. I will miss his funny corny jokes. Most of all, I will miss his friendship. Maybe the summer will pass quickly.

I am tired of dad coming to my room at night. I don't like what he does to me. I don't like having to do things to him. It seems like Dad loves Kathy more than me. He jokes with her and sometimes hugs her in front of me.

When this happens, I can feel the anger stir within my body. I want to scream. I want to yell. I want it to stop.

He never hugs me or tells me he loves me in front of her. Instead, he sneaks to my room. He told me I would always be his special little girl. But I'm not. He lied to me.

Junior is allowed to come home every other weekend. Thank God! At least I have someone to whom I can talk. We always manage to spend some time, talking about Kathy. I let him know I am not allowed to do anything.

I wish I could talk to him about Dad. When he's home, he spends as little time as possible at the house. Many times he and Kathy get into arguments. Sometimes they get into fistfights.

Junior has really filled out. He has muscles and is strong. If Kathy hits him, he is not afraid to hit her back. I like it, when Junior yells at or hits her back. I think about all the times she would beat him, and he wasn't able to defend himself. I wish, I could yell at her. I wish, I could hit her back. I can't. I'm afraid of her. Dad is of no help.

He doesn't say a word. He sits and smokes cigarette after cigarette and says nothing.

Today, Diane Meier comes to the house. She and Kathy sit at the kitchen table. Kathy complains to her about Junior's behavior, when he is home. I hear Kathy tell her she doesn't have any support or freedom.

I think to myself, "You have more freedom than I, I have to do everything around here."

When the woman comes to the house, I am usually cleaning, cooking or taking care of the boys. I say nothing to her.

One day she comes to the house in the afternoon. Dad and Kathy are home.

I am sitting on the front steps of the neighbor's house, when I see her park her car across the street and get out. She walks across the street.

I'm hoping, maybe she will talk to me.

She carries a big leather bag over her shoulder and looks in my direction. She says, "Hi," then continues to walk toward the apartment.

I say nothing. I want so much for her to talk to me. I hear Kathy call out my name. I go running. Kathy, Dad and Diane Meier are sitting at the kitchen table.

Kathy says, "Take the boys outside."

I do as I am told.

I stand at the side of the house by the open window in the living room to try to hear what is being said inside.

Michael and Joey are laughing. Chasing one another around the yard.

I can't hear what is being said. I wish the boys would be quiet.

Michael pulls on my leg. He wants me to chase him. I look down at him and say, "I'm going to get you."

Michael turns and runs towards the back yard, laughing.

I give up on trying to hear what is being said. I run after the boys.

They laugh. I pull Michael to the ground. He's on his back. I tickle him. He laughs.

Joey says, "Me too."

I pull him to the ground, put him on his back and tickle him.

Both boys laugh. Then tell me to stop.

I stop.

Then they scream out, "More. More." Both the boys are a great escape for me. They don't scream, yell, or hit me. When I give them a hug, I get one back.

In July, Kathy goes into the hospital for a hysterectomy. Dad tells me she will be there for about a week.

I will be taking care of both the boys. I am so excited, thinking to myself, "Maybe, I can talk Dad into kicking her out. I'll tell him I will take care of the boys."

As the days pass and it gets closer to the time Kathy goes into the hospital, she gets more demanding. It seems that I don't have a moment to myself because she is complaining all the time.

The day has arrived for her to leave for the hospital. It is difficult for me to hide my excitement. I manage to keep it under control. I just want her to leave.

To make things look good I need to let Kathy know I will miss her. I don't want to do this, but know if she thinks I am happy about her going into the hospital, I will pay for it, once she comes home. I think about what I will say to her. I'll tell her I will miss her. I'll tell her I will take care of the boys. It won't all be a lie. I will take care of the boys.

Kathy has her suitcase packed. Dad is ready to take her. Kathy looks sad and worried.

I look at her and tell her I will miss her. I tell her I will take care of both Michael and Joey. I must remember to ask God to forgive me for lying. I won't miss her.

Dad says, "It is time to leave." He picks up the suitcase and heads out the door.

Kathy hugs both the boys. She doesn't say a word to me.

Dad yells, "Come on."

She pulls the door open, and out she goes.

I am relieved. She is finally gone.

Dad told me a couple weeks ago that he had a surprise for me, while Kathy was in the hospital.

I asked him what it was, but he wouldn't tell me.

He told me it would be a special time for us.

I wonder what it is. Maybe, he is going to tell me he realizes Kathy is so mean. Maybe, he is going to tell me he is going to kick her out.

Kathy has been gone for two days. The house is so peaceful.

Michael and Joey seem to be enjoying the calm as much as I am. The boys get up in the morning, have breakfast, then spend time in the backyard, playing. Neither one of them have asked me about her.

I wonder if they are just as happy to get a break from her as I am. I'm fixing lunch for the boys and myself. I go into the refrigerator, notice a six pack of beer, which I don't remember seeing yesterday. We never have beer in the house. I wonder, why it is there.

I've only seen dad drink once, when we lived in the country. It seems so very long ago. I'll have to ask dad about it. He should be home for lunch soon.

Michael, Joey and I are sitting at the table, eating lunch, as dad walks in the door.

He says, "Hi."

I ask him, "Do you want me to make you a sandwich?"

He says, "I can fix my own. Sit and finish eating. Kathy's surgery went well."

I ask, "When she will be coming home?"

He says, "Not for a few more days."

I let him know I saw beer in the refrigerator. "What is it for?"

He looks at me and says, "It is part of the surprise I have for you."

I ask, "What do you mean?"

Dad says, "You will find out tonight."

We've finished lunch, and Dad goes back up to the hospital.

As I'm clearing the table, I hear a knock at the door.

It is Jeanette, a neighbor from across the street. She asks if everything is okay?

I let her know Kathy's surgery went well and she will be home in a few days.

Jeanette tells me she told Kathy she would check in on us.

The boys are running around the apartment. They aren't doing anything wrong, just having fun.

I let Jeanette know everything is fine, and thank her for stopping. She leaves.

I tell the boys it is time to take a nap. Hugs and kisses are given to them. A story is read. Both Michael and Joey are finally down for a nap.

It is break time for me. The apartment is quiet. I sit on the couch, thinking about what Dad had said earlier. I wonder why beer would be a part of my surprise.

I don't give it too much more thought. Instead, I turn on the television. I go from one channel to the next. My choices are a game show, a soap opera or Hollywood Matinee. I don't like game shows. I don't like soap operas. I watch the movie, until the boys awaken.

Michael and Joey are in the backyard.

Dad is fixing dinner when he tells me he won't be going to the hospital to see Kathy tonight, because he was there most of the day.

This makes me very happy. He will be home all night. Maybe, I can talk to him about Kathy.

After dinner, I put things away. While I am doing the dishes, I can hear the boys in the other room with dad.

Michael is laughing.

Joey says, "Get me."

It is so nice to hear laughter, instead of yelling and screaming. I stand at the sink and think about Kathy coming home from the hospital. I feel my body become tense, just thinking about her.

Both Michael and Joey are laughing. Their giggles distract me from my thoughts of Kathy. The dishes are done. I look around the kitchen, and everything appears to be in order. I walk into the living room.

The boys are sitting on the couch with dad. Michael is on one side of him and Joey on the other. They are watching television.

As I look at the three of them, it reminds me of the times, when Junior and I were younger. We use to sit on the couch with Dad and watch television. All three of them look so relaxed, content, and happy.

I have just put Michael and Joey to bed. The apartment is quiet.

I am walking from dad and Kathy's bedroom into the living room. Dad is sitting on the couch.

I look at him.

He says, "Come. Sit next to me."

I walk towards the couch, noticing a can of beer on the coffee table. An empty glass is sitting next to it.

I plop down next to Dad.

He says, "This is our special night."

I turn look at him and say, "What do you mean?"

He says, "Tonight you become a woman."

I say, "I don't understand."

Dad reaches for the empty glass, then the can of beer. He pours it, then hands it to me.

I stare at him, not sure what I am supposed to do.

He says, "Drink it."

I say, "If Kathy finds out, we'll get into trouble."

Dad says, "She will never find out."

I bring the glass to my lips. I smell the beer and take a sip. It tastes bitter. I take another sip. I like it. I sit back on the couch. As I continue to take sips, I talk to Dad. "I don't want Kathy to come back. I am tired of her beating me. I am tired of her being so mean. It is quieter without her around."

He says, "She has to stay."

I ask, "Why?"

He says, "She has to take care of Michael and Joey."

I say, "She doesn't do anything around here. I am the one who takes care of the boys."

He says, "She has to stay."

I ask, "Do you love her more than me?"

Dad says, "You will always be my special little girl."

I ask, "Why do you let her get away with being so mean?"

Dad doesn't say anything.

I ask, "Are you afraid of her?" I look at dad.

He looks at me and says, "Yes."

I continue to drink the glass of beer. My body begins to feel a little numb. My thoughts wander. I feel lightheaded.

Dad moves closer to me.

I finish drinking the beer and put the empty glass on the coffee table.

Dad puts his arm around me.

I turn towards him, putting my arms around him. I squeeze and can hear his heart beating. I tell Dad, "I love you."

He says, "I love you too."

As we are holding one another Dad says, "We are going to sleep together tonight."

I say, "Really."

He says, "Yes."

Dad stands up, looking down at me and reaching for my hand. He pulls me up from the couch.

Hand in hand, we walk from the living room to his bedroom.

It is dark. As we stand next to the bed, dad disrobes me, pulling my top up over my head. Instead of placing it on the bed, he throws it on the floor, then moves his hands down my shoulders and finally to my waistline.

I stand in silence, not knowing what to do or what to say.

He uses both his hands to pull my pants down over my waist and down my legs. He looks at me, caresses my face and says, "Climb in bed."

God, the bed is so much bigger than mine is. I'm on my back. Dad is next to me. I can feel the warmth of his skin.

He doesn't have any clothes on. He stretches his body over mine, kisses me. His lips feel warm. Dad whispers in my ear, "I love you."

My arms are wrapped around him. I feel his strong muscles. I hold on to him. His skin feels warm.

He spreads my legs open.

I can feel his penis against my leg. It feels warm. It feels hard.

Dad's breathing is getting deeper. He's not saying anything.

I wish he would talk to me. I feel his penis entering my vagina. My body becomes very tense. God, it hurts. I try to pull away. I can't move.

Dad is on top of me. He pushes it deeper and deeper. It feels like his penis is going to come out of my mouth. It hurts so badly. I want to scream. I want to cry. I want to push him off me. I don't scream. I don't cry. I hold on to him as tightly as I can and hope it will be over soon. Dad pulls his penis out of me. He squirts all that awful stuff that comes out onto my stomach.

I can feel the warmth of it, as it lands. I smell it. My stomach feels sticky. My vagina hurts.

Dad lays next to me, pulling me close to him.

I'm on my side facing him.

He has his arm around me.

My face is touching his chest, which feels wet.

He's not breathing as deeply as he was, when he was on top of me. Dad whispers, "You are a woman."

I ask, "What do you mean?"

Dad tells me, "You are no longer a virgin. I love you."

I lift my head from dad's chest, look at him and say, "I love you too."

Dad falls asleep.

I lay next to him for what seems to be hours. I think about what we just did. I wonder how many times we will do this. I'm hoping not again. I have all that sticky awful stuff on my stomach. I reach for the sheet, wiping the stuff off. I hate the smell of it, the way it feels and the taste of it. I wonder if this means I won't have to put his penis in my mouth. My vagina still hurts. It feels like his penis is still inside me.

I think to myself, "If it is going to hurt like this, I'd rather have his penis in my mouth. At least it won't hurt."

I lay on my stomach next to him, reaching for the pillow and hugging it tightly. I talk to God. I ask him to make my vagina stop hurting. I ask him not to let dad put his penis inside me again. I tell God I know dad didn't mean to hurt me. I tell him dad loves me.

It is August. The summer is passing quickly. In less than a month I go back to school. I am looking forward to being away from the house during the day.

Junior is home for the weekend.

Dad and Kathy have taken the boys with them to do some shopping.

It is a Saturday afternoon. Junior and I hang out. We're standing in the living room next to the couch. I fill him in on all the things Kathy has said and done. I tell him that ever since she came home from the hospital, she complains about the tiniest things. I let him know she has gotten into some big arguments with dad.

Junior asks, "About what?"

I tell him, "She has become very jealous of me. One day Dad bought me some Clearasil for my acne, and she had a fit. She told him he cares more about me than her." I let Junior know dad still buys the Clearasil for me, but he sneaks it to me without her knowing. I tell him, "I can't

125

stand it at home! The only time I get to leave the house is to go to the store. And when I do this, either Dad or Kathy watch me."

Junior laughs and says, "She hasn't changed."

I say, "You're right."

Junior grabs me, pushes me onto the couch then jumps on top of me. He tries to kiss me. I push him away. He resists.

I look at him and say, "Get off of me now, or I will kill you!"

Junior says, "Okay. Okay. Okay." He gets up and stands next to the couch.

I stand up and stare at him.

He says, "I was only kidding, Sis."

I look at him and say, "Don't ever touch me again!"

He says, "Come on. Don't be mad at me."

I say, "I'm not mad at you. Just don't touch me."

It's Sunday afternoon. Junior has to return to Crane Hill. He tells me he'll be home in a couple weeks. Although, we always tell one another we'll write, we never do.

He looks at me before leaving and says, "I love you, Sis."

I look at him and say, "I love you, too."

He leaves.

Later that day I think about him. Before he came home this weekend, I thought of telling him about Dad and I. It's probably a good thing I didn't. After all I promised dad I would tell no one. That includes Junior. I can't believe he tried to pin me down. I can't believe he tried to kiss me. At least, he got up off of me. I think I scared him. I hope so.

Chapter Thirteen

Freedom

The next three months would be unbearable. I would make a decision that would change my life forever. It would be one of the hardest, wisest and healthiest decisions I would ever make.

It is September of 1970. School starts tomorrow. I have some new clothes and I'll be away from the house most of the day. Life is good. I am excited.

During the summer, Margaret stopped a few times at the house. Once, to ask if I could go swimming. I couldn't. I had to take care of the boys. Another time she stopped and hung out for a while. This was disastrous.

Kathy was in one of her moods. On this particular day, she was very demanding and started yelling at me in front of Margaret.

I could tell my friend felt very uncomfortable. I was so embarrassed. Why did she have to yell at me in front of her? Why couldn't she wait, until after Margaret was gone? That would be asking too much of her. I know better. She only thinks about herself. This was the last time Margaret came to the house.

There were times during the summer that I would be outside with the boys, and Margaret or Mark would walk by. We would wave to one another. Although, my encounters with them throughout the summer were few, I thought about them often. I hope they'll be on the corner, waiting for me in morning.

It is 6:15 a.m. Dad wakes me up, just before he leaves for work. He tells me, "Have a good day."

The apartment is quiet. It is still dark. I get out of bed and walk through the living room into the kitchen, which isn't dark.

Dad has left the bathroom door ajar with the light on.

I hear the sound of birds chirping outside. I wonder if the birds are as happy as I am.

Kathy, Michael and Joey are still sleeping, so I move around the apartment quietly. I don't want to wake them, especially Kathy, who would ruin my morning. I walk into the bathroom to brush my teeth, wash my face and comb my hair. I quietly walk through the kitchen, then the living room and into my bedroom. I don't turn on the light. I make my bed, take my pajamas off, reach for my clothes and put them on. Then I hurry back out into the kitchen.

It is getting late, and I still need to make a sandwich for lunch. I think about opening the refrigerator to get some lunchmeat. I decide not to. If I open the refrigerator, Kathy might see the light. Instead, I make a peanut butter and jelly sandwich.

I look at the clock. It is 7:10 a.m. I rush to wrap my sandwich, placing it in a sandwich bag, along with a piece of fruit. I walk back into the bathroom to look in the mirror. My hair won't stay in place. I reach for the comb, running it through my hair one more time before leaving. I turn the bathroom light off, walk into the kitchen, I reach for my lunch from the kitchen table and leave. I notice it has gotten light out. I close the door quietly. Making as little noise as possible.

As I walk up the street, I hope, Margaret and Mark are waiting for me at the corner. I can still hear the birds chirping. I turn my head in that direction, but don't see any. I continue to walk up the street, listening. The sound of the birds becomes music to my ears.

As I get closer to the corner, I can see both Margaret and Mark. I speed up my walk to get to the corner quickly. I grin at Margaret.

She smiles and says, "Hi."

I look at them and say, "Hi. I have missed you guys. I'm glad school has finally started."

The three of us begin our mile walk to school. Margaret and Mark tell me what fun things they did over the summer. I listen to them.

Mark tells me he worked at a local restaurant, washing dishes. He goes on to tell me he didn't like it, but enjoyed the money he earned.

Margaret tells me she spent a lot of her time at the Girls' Club, the local pools and just hanging out at home.

It is my turn to share, but fun was not a part of my summer. I didn't get to go swimming. I tell them I didn't do anything exciting. I took care of my brothers.

Mark asks, "You didn't get to do anything fun?"

I say, "No."

Mark asks, "Why is she so mean?"

I say, "I don't know."

We are almost to school. Although we go to the same Junior High School, none of us are in the same classes. I tell both Margaret and Mark to have a nice day.

Margaret asks, "Are we going to walk home together?"

I say, "Meet me out front after school. Remember, I have to get home right after school."

Margaret says, "Okay."

The three of us enter the school. We look for our home-rooms, traveling in opposite directions.

As I walk to my homeroom, I think about Margaret and Mark. I am so glad they waited for me at the corner. It is so nice to see them again. I hope we can walk to and from school every day. I won't tell Kathy or Dad. It's none of their business. They don't need to know. Margaret and Mark are MY friends.

I've been in school about three weeks. Margaret, Mark and I continue to walk to school together each morning. Margaret becomes involved with after school activities. It isn't often she walks home from school with me. Mark still has his part-time job as a dishwasher. He works at the restaurant a couple nights a week. He tells me he doesn't have time to become involved with after school activities. I'm glad. I enjoy walking home from school with him.

I begin to feel resentful. My life is so different from all the other kids. They get to take their time, walking home after school. I have to rush. If I'm not home at exactly 3:15p.m. I get a beating. I'd like to be able to get involved with after school activities.

Margaret says she has a lot of fun.

I want to have fun! I'd like to say something to Kathy and dad, but I know better. If I say something to Kathy, she will think I am sassing her, then yell, call me names, say mean things and hit me. I'm not willing to let that happen. It already occurs often enough.

It seems, like dad really never hears what I am saying. Sure he listens, but it seems like all I say goes in one ear and out the other. It has become clear to me ever since that warm summer night in July, when I entered womanhood, dad is only interested in me for the sexual things I do for him. He knows that Kathy is mean, yet he lets her get away with it. He says he loves me. But I wonder. Dad didn't do anything to protect Junior. He chose Kathy and had Junior sent away. That man doesn't do anything to protect me. He just takes from me and gives very little back. It has become obvious to me that he loves her more. I begin to wonder what will happen to me.

I begin to dread the weekends. I have no break. At least during the week, I am at school a good part of the day. I get to see Margaret and Mark. No one at school is mean to me. I guess, things could be worse. I could be home all the time.

Dad continues to come into my bedroom at night, while Kathy is taking a bath. This one particular night when he comes, I'm sitting on the edge of my bed. He puts his penis in my mouth.

I'm shaking it. I squeeze and bite down on it at the same time.

Dad pulls away. "Be careful."

I say, "Oh I'm sorry." I did it intentionally. I wish the damn thing would fall off. Dad sticks it back in my mouth. I squeeze it, shake it and am careful not to hurt him again. The awful stuff comes out of it. God, how I hate that taste.

He pulls his penis out of my mouth, puts it back into his pants, zips his zipper, then he walks out into the living room, sits on the couch and watches television. He acts like nothing has happened.

My mouth tastes awful. I wish, I could get up to brush my teeth. But I know better. I will have to wait until morning. I lay in bed, thinking about dad. I don't want him to touch me any more. I don't want to put his penis in my mouth. I wonder what night it will be that he will put his penis inside me again. I don't want him to do that ever again; it hurts too much.

Tonight, I think about running away. If I leave, dad won't be able to touch me. If I leave, I will be away from Kathy.

I think about Michael and Joey. They rely on me so much. If I leave, will Kathy beat them? If I leave, who will care for and protect them?

I have to do something, because I can't stand it any more. I feel like I am going to explode. I want to leave. I'm tired of taking care of everyone. I'm tired of having to think about every move I make. I'm tired of always worrying about everyone else.

I talk to God. "Please, help me get out of here."

Mark and I are walking home from school. The air is crisp. The sun is shining. It's a beautiful October afternoon. I'm only about two and a half blocks away from the apartment.

Mark looks at me and says, "Let's sit under the oak tree."

I say, "I have to get home."

Mark says, "Just for a minute. I want to give you something."

We walk towards the oak tree. I have passed it daily on my walks to and from school. It's tall with many branches, which look so sturdy and strong.

Mark says, "Come and sit."

So I sit next to him on the ground, leaning my back against the tree and listening to the traffic in the distance behind us.

Mark takes the medallion off that he wears around his neck. "I want you to have this."

He places it around my neck.

I don't know what to say. No one has ever given me a gift like this before. I can feel my face getting warm. I wonder if I am blushing. I look at Mark and say, "Thank you."

He smiles.

I say, "I have to go."

We both stand up and continue our walk home. I say good bye to Mark in front of his house and tell him I will see him Monday morning.

I turn away and continue my walk home. I speed up my pace. God, I hope I'm not late.

As I hurry, I think about Mark. He is so nice. I can't believe he gave me his medallion. I feel the chain attached to it encircling my neck. I touch it. The medal is hard and round, about the size of an orange.

Oh no, I must be late. I see Kathy standing in front of the apartment. If she beats me, it doesn't matter. Spending a few extra minutes with Mark was worth it.

I'm standing in front of the apartment. She looks at me and says, "You're late.

Where were you? "

I say, "I was walking home from school."

She says, "Get in the house."

I move quickly down the stairs and into the apartment.

Kathy is right behind me.

I hear the neighbor next door say something to her. They continue to talk.

I hope she stays outside, until Dad gets home. I look at the clock that hangs on the kitchen wall. It says 3:25 p.m. I think to myself, "I'm late, but not that late." I better get the coffee going for Dad. I don't bother changing out of my school clothes. I'll do it after the coffee is made.

The coffee is brewing. Kathy walks in the door. She looks at me and says, "What is that around your neck?"

I say, "What?"

She walks towards me.

I don't know what to do. I want to run. My body doesn't move. I feel frozen.

She is standing right in front of me. I brace myself, waiting for the first anticipated slap across my face. Instead of hitting me, she reaches for the medallion, pulls it with great force, and breaks the chain, as she yanks it from around my neck. Clutching it, she demands to know, "Where did you get this?" Raising her voice she says, "You're a whore! You bitch! Where did you get this?"

I can feel my body shaking. I know I better give her an answer. I say, "Mark gave it to me."

She shouts, "You bitch!"

I'm so mad. How dare she call me name after name. How dare she rip the medallion from my neck? I look at her and say, "You're the bitch!" I thought, for sure she was really going to give it to me. I've never called her a name before.

She stares as if though she is in shock.

A minute passes.

She looks at me and says, "Go to your room."

I walk through the kitchen, then the living room and into my bedroom, closing the door. I can't believe she didn't hit me. I change into my play clothes, then sit on the bed. I hope dad gets home soon. I hear Kathy yell for me. I stand up, thinking to myself, "Oh no, I'm going to get it." When I open my door, she is sitting on the couch.

I look at her.

She says, "Get your ass in the kitchen and peel some potatoes for dinner."

I go directly to the kitchen. I'm sitting at the table, peeling the potatoes.

She walks into the kitchen and looks at me.

Oh, God what is she going to do!

She clutches the medallion in her hand and says, "You'll never get it back."

I say nothing.

Dad walks in the door.

I say to myself, "He is finally home."

I feel safe.

Kathy will say mean things to me, when Dad is home; but she never hits me in front of him.

Tonight, as I lay in bed, I think about Mark. I wonder, what he will say, when I tell him what she did. I bet he'll be upset. What will he say? What will he think? Will he be mad at me?

I can no longer stand living here. I have made up my mind to run away. As soon as I have a plan, I am going to leave. I'd rather live on the streets than like this.

I will let Margaret and Mark know of my plan on Monday morning. I will swear them to secrecy. I know they won't say a word to anyone.

Monday morning has finally arrived. The weekend seemed to pass so slowly. Off to school I go. I meet Margaret and Mark at the corner. We begin our walk to school.

The first few minutes, we walk in silence.

I am nervous about telling Mark about the medallion. I'm nervous about telling them I am going to run away.

As we are walking up the hill, I say, "Kathy took the medallion."

Mark looks at me and says, "What? "

I say, "She took the medallion."

Mark asks, "When? "

I say, "She ripped it off my neck on Friday, when I got home."

135

Margaret says, "She is so mean. How can you stand it?"

I say, "I can't! I'm going to run away."

Margaret looks at me and asks, "Where will you go?"

I say, "I don't know."

Mark asks, "When? "

I say, "Soon."

Margaret says, "She will look for you."

I say, "I can't stand living in the house any longer. She is so mean. She treats me so badly."

Margaret says, "I know."

I say, "You can't say a word to anyone. Promise!"

They look at me and swear to secrecy. They promise not to tell anyone.

I know they won't.

They too know how mean she is. They didn't tell me not to run away.

It feels good to have shared with them. Now, to come up with a plan.

It is Friday. The three of us are walking to school. I let Margaret and Mark know I won't be walking to school with them any more.

Margaret asks, "Why?"

I say, "I'm going to run away."

Margaret asks, "When?"

I say, "I will leave in the middle of the night, when everyone is sleeping."

Margaret asks, "What if she catches you?"

I say, "She won't."

We continue our walk to school. Not very many words are spoken.

I feel, as if though I am saying good-bye to my best friends.

We are in front of the school. I look at them and say, "I will miss you."

Mark asks, "Are we walking home together?"

I say, "Yes."

Margaret says, "I am walking home with you, too."

I say, "I'll meet you in front of the school."

The three of us go our separate ways. We will come together again at the end of the school day.

The dismissal bell rings. The school day has ended.

I walk out of my homeroom, down the hall and out the big wooden doors. I feel the concrete steps beneath my feet, as I walk to the front of the building.

While I stand, waiting for my two friends, I reflect upon my time spent at the school. No one was ever mean to me. I really enjoyed and liked all my teachers. School and my teachers were my safe haven of rest during the week.

Margaret and Mark appear. We begin our walk home. Neither one of us say very much.

As we are passing the oak tree, I smile. I remember the day Mark and I sat beneath its strong branches.

Margaret says, "Take my phone number. Call, if you need anything."

I look at her and say, "Thanks."

We are standing in front of their house. The three of us look at one another. It seems neither one of us knows what to say.

I break the silence and say, "I have to go. I don't want to be late. " I turn and walk away.

I hear Margaret say, "Good-bye."

I don't turn around, but continue down the street. I will miss them.

It is Sunday evening. I'm putting the boys to bed.

Michael has been very clingy all weekend. He wants me to rub his back, instead of just tucking him in.

I do, as he requests. He lies on his stomach. I rub his back very gently. His eyes close.

I continue to rub his back in an up and down motion. As I am rubbing, I think about the boys.

Tonight I will leave. I wonder if they will miss me. I wonder if they will be okay.

I stop rubbing Michael's back. He doesn't open his eyes. He is asleep. I kiss him on his head. "I love you." I stand up.

Joey is on the top bunk. He is asleep. I kiss him on the cheek. "I love you too." Before leaving their room, I silently ask God to watch over them. I can feel the tears in my eyes. I take a deep breath, wipe my eyes and walk out of their room.

I lay in my bed wide-awake. The house is quiet.

Kathy and Dad went to bed a couple hours ago. I wonder if they are asleep. I decide to take my pajamas off and get dressed. Before going to bed, I put a set of clothes under my bed. I reach for them and put them on.

Then I think, "What if they wake up." I scare myself and begin to get nervous. So I sit on my bed to think about what I am doing. I think about why I am doing it. I decide it is worth the risk of getting caught.

Over the weekend I was able to sneak some clothing into a garbage bag. I hid it under my bed. Earlier today, I was able to sneak it out of my room and hide it in back of one of the garbage cans outside. I can't forget to grab it. I will need those few things to keep warm.

I sit on my bed and go over the plan of escape in my head. I will crawl across the living room floor, on into the kitchen, then out the door.

I can feel my body become tense; my heart pounds; my hands are all sweaty. I take a deep breath then decide it is time to go. I stand in my doorway to listen. It is still quiet. I'm sure they aren't going to wake up.

I get on my hands and knees, lay on my stomach, and crawl across the living room floor. My head hits one of the legs to the coffee table. I lay there in silence. I don't make a sound. Then, I continue to crawl across the floor, until I reach the kitchen. The door is only about three feet away. I stand up as I reach for the door handle. I use my other hand to unlock the dead bolt. I pull the door open and walk outside.

After pulling the door shut, I walk to the trashcans. I grab the bag hidden behind them. I run up the three concrete stairs that lead to the street and make a right. I swing the trash bag over my shoulder as I walk up the street. When I pass Margaret and Marks house, I smile.

I hurry to the park and climb the many stairs. I am about half way up. No one will find me here. I am safe. I put my trash bag on a step, then sit on the one just below it. I lean back, resting my head on the bag.

It is dark. Quiet. A chill's in the air. I sure am glad I thought to bring some warm clothes. I look up into the night sky to admire a few bright shining stars. Some are brighter than others. I continue to gaze up at the stars, for what seems to be a long time. I so much appreciate the silence, the peacefulness and the beauty of the twinkling stars.

I take a deep breath, stare into the night sky one more time, then shout, "I'm free, I'm free! Thank you, God!"

139

Resources

Child Help USA
15757 North Seventy 8th Street
Scottsdale, Arizona 85260
1-800-422-4453
> Offers a 24—hour crisis hot line, national information and referral Network for support groups, therapists, and for reporting suspected abuse

The National Committee to Prevent Child Abuse (NCPCA)
P.O. Box 2866
Chicago, IL 60690
1-800-556-2722
> Headquartered in Chicago, is a nonprofit organization with the goal of preventing child abuse in all forms. NCPCA promotes public education through its national media campaign, a catalog of publications, and training and technical assistance. Chapters of the national organization are located throughout the United States.

Child Welfare League of America
440 First Street, NW, Suite 310
Washington, DC 20001-2085
1-202-638-2952
> Headquartered in Washington, DC. The Child Welfare League of America is a 75 year-old association of nearly 800 public and private, nonprofit agencies that serve abused, neglected and abandoned children, youth and their families. CWLA plays a major advocacy role

on Capitol Hill, developing guidelines for the provision of child welfare services, conducting research and training, and is the world's largest publisher of child welfare materials.

Survivors of Incest Anonymous
P.O. Box 190
Benson, Maryland 21018-9998
1-410-893-3322
www.siawso.org
Is a nonprofit organization with the goal to help survivors to connect with one another and carry the message of recovery to those who still suffer. It serves as a headquarters for 300 plus SIA meetings in the United States and around the world.

New York State Child Abuse and Maltreatment Reporting Center
P. O. Box 4480
Albany, New York 12204
1-800-342-3720
A 24-hour hotline that is utilized for making reports in regards to abused and maltreated children living within New York State.

RAINN (Rape, Abuse & Incest National Network)
635-B Pennsylvania Ave., SE
Washington, DC 20003
1-800-656-4673
www.rainn.org
A 24-hour hotline offering confidential counseling and referrals.

Cathy Brochu

The International Newsletter for Woman Survivors of Childhood Sexual Abuse
The Healing Woman Foundation
P.O. Box Z8040
San Jose, CA 95159
408-246-1788
http://www.healingwoman.org
Offers publications and support.

National Organization on Male Survivor Victimization
5505 Connecticut Ave. NW
Washington, DC 20015-2601
1-800-738-4181
www.malesurvivor.org
A nonprofit organization dedicated to healing male survivors of sexual abuse.

VOICES in Action, Inc.
P.O. Box 148309
Chicago, IL 60614
773-327-1500
http://voices-action.org
Offers referrals to therapists, self-help groups, agencies, and legal resources.

Keynotes, Seminars and Workshops

The goal of Cathy's distinctive presentations is to motivate individuals. Her intent is to encourage individuals to move beyond barriers, to move from low self-esteem to self-worth and to find purposeful fulfillment. Additionally, Cathy offers workshops and seminars for those in the human service, educational and law enforcement field.

Let us continue to work towards empowering individuals, families and communities with the hope that WE can pave the path to a healthier, happier future for the children of tomorrow.

For additional, specific information you can contact Cathy at:

Cathy Brochu
Espouse
P. O. Box 158
Jamesville, New York 13078-9536
E-mail: C.Brochu@juno.com
http://web.A-Znet.com/makana

Cathy Brochu

About The Author

Cathy Brochu no longer lives her life shamed, fearful, isolated or stripped of self-esteem. She speaks openly and honestly about her thirteen-year experience growing-up in an incestuous family. She has worked in the field of Child Welfare for more than twenty-eight years working directly with victims, perpetrators and families. She has heard the endless stories and cries for help.

Cathy holds a Bachelor of Arts Degree, is a clinical hypnotherapist and has been trained in acupuncture detoxification for alcoholism. In 1995, she was the recipient of the Women of Courage Award presented by the Syracuse Commission for Women for setting an example in overcoming the odds and speaking out about incest. She has been featured in newspapers throughout Central New York for her work initiating and facilitating support groups for adult incest survivors. She also lectures to second year medical students on the importance of knowing what to look for, what to ask, and what to do for a potential victim of child sexual abuse. She trains lay and professional human service staff in the area of child sexual abuse and has been the guest speaker for numerous nonprofit agencies. She has committed herself to empowering and strengthening individuals, families and communities to move beyond hopelessness to becoming leaders of their own lives.

A portion of the proceeds through the selling of this book will be used to establish Support Groups within communities at no cost to the recipient.

Cathy is currently working on the second part of her trilogy series, *New Beginnings.*

Printed in the United States
106770LV00004B